英　语

主　编　柯　强　冯卫东
副主编　柯于大
参　编　柯文敏　万翠　周兰萍　曹红霞

北京理工大学出版社
BEIJING INSTITUTE OF TECHNOLOGY PRESS

版权专有 侵权必究

图书在版编目（CIP）数据

英语 / 柯强，冯卫东主编 .—北京：北京理工大学出版社，2019.8 重印
ISBN 978-7-5682-5997-2

Ⅰ.①英… Ⅱ.①柯…②冯… Ⅲ.①英语课–中等专业学校–教材 Ⅳ.① G634.411

中国版本图书馆 CIP 数据核字（2018）第 172883 号

出版发行 / 北京理工大学出版社有限责任公司
社　　址 / 北京市海淀区中关村南大街 5 号
邮　　编 / 100081
电　　话 /（010）68914775（总编室）
　　　　　（010）82562903（教材售后服务热线）
　　　　　（010）68948351（其他图书服务热线）
网　　址 / http：//www.bitpress.com.cn
经　　销 / 全国各地新华书店
印　　刷 / 定州市新华印刷有限公司
开　　本 / 787 毫米 ×1092 毫米　1/16
印　　张 / 9　　　　　　　　　　　　　　　责任编辑 / 张荣君
字　　数 / 220 千字　　　　　　　　　　　　文案编辑 / 张荣君
版　　次 / 2019 年 8 月第 1 版第 4 次印刷　　责任校对 / 周瑞红
定　　价 / 29.80 元　　　　　　　　　　　　责任印制 / 边心超

图书出现印装质量问题，请拨打售后服务热线，本社负责调换

前　言

2015年7月,《教育部关于深化职业教育教学改革全面提高人才培养质量的若干意见》指出,"发挥人文学科的独特育人优势,加强公共基础课与专业课间的相互融通和配合,注重学生文化素质、科学素养、综合职业能力和可持续发展能力培养,为学生实现更高质量就业和职业生涯更好发展奠定基础"。语文、数学、英语是中等职业学校学生必修的公共文化基础课。其任务是为专业知识的学习和职业技能的培养奠定基础,满足学生职业生涯发展的需要,促进终身学习。

可见,中职学生学好公共文化基础课非常有必要,特别是语文、数学、英语。一段时间以来,有的不重视文化基础课的教学,认为中职生文化基础差,学不学无所谓,就是学好了也没有多大作用等等"无用论";有的不切实际,盲目提高文化课基础课要求;有的随意削弱文化基础课,不开、少开。把文化基础课等同于一般培训机构,只重视专业课学习,完全忽视文化基础课的学习。

结合我校办学实际、学生学情,我们发现,中职新生普遍存在文化基础课薄弱的现象。基于促进学生终身发展、可持续发展的需要,使学生在原有基础上筑牢基础;基于共同基础和多样选择相结合的需要,确保中职生必需的文化素养。同时,贯彻统一性和灵活性的原则,实施与评价不搞一刀切。为此,我们组织一线文化课教师编写了这套系列初高中衔接教材。

编写文化基础课衔接教材,是我们的第一次尝试。由于编者水平有限,书中难免有不妥之处,敬请读者给予批评指正。

编者
2018年5月

目 录

Unit One　Families ································· 1
　　单元复习 ····································· 5
Unit Two　Animals ································· 8
　　单元复习 ····································· 12
Unit Three　Getting Around ························· 16
　　单元复习 ····································· 20
Unit Four　Sports ································· 24
　　单元复习 ····································· 30
Unit Five　Go Shopping ····························· 34
　　单元复习 ····································· 38
Unit Six　Holidays ································· 41
　　单元复习 ····································· 46
Unit Seven　Water ································· 50
　　单元复习 ····································· 57
Unit Eight　Science ································· 60
　　单元复习 ····································· 64
Unit Nine　Medicine ································· 66
　　单元复习 ····································· 70
Unit Ten　Childhood ································· 73
　　单元复习 ····································· 76
Unit Eleven　Computer ····························· 79
　　单元复习 ····································· 84
Unit Twelve　Work ································· 87
　　单元复习 ····································· 93

Unit Thirteen　Film ·· 96
　　单元复习 ·· 101
Unit Fourteen　The Olympic Games ··· 103
　　单元复习 ·· 107
Unit Fifteen　Health ··· 109
　　单元复习 ·· 114
Unit Sixteen　Pollution ··· 117
　　单元复习 ·· 122
Unit Seventeen　News ·· 125
　　单元复习 ·· 128
Unit Eighteen　Advertising ·· 131
　　单元复习 ·· 136

Unit One   Families

Warming up

Which looks like your family?

1. Discussion.

(1) How many people are there in your family?

(2) Who are they?

(3) How many brothers and sisters do you have?

(4) Does your grandfather have many sons and daughters?

(5) Whose family is the biggest, yours, your father's, or your grandfather's?

2. Pair work: Read the following dialogue with your partner.

A: How many people are there in your family?

B: Five—my parents, elder sister, younger brother and I.

A: Which city are you from?

B: I'm from Xuzhou.

A: What do your parents do?

B: My father is a teacher. He teaches physics. My mother works in a nursery. She teaches children how to sing and speak clearly.

A: How about your brother, your sister and you?

B: My elder sister is a nurse. My younger brother is at a middle school. I am working in a computer company.

A: Best wishes to your family.

Families in the Future

In recent years, families are becoming smaller. Fifty years ago, a family of five or six members was common. In 1970, the size of the average family in the United States was 3.1 persons, and now the average family size is about 2.8 persons. At the same time, people are now living longer. For example, in the last ten years, the number of people over 65 years of age has increased 28 per cent. The average age of people in the United States is now over 30.

As a result of smaller families and more old people, life will change in many ways. If we have fewer children, we will need fewer schools. We will also need fewer teachers. But many older people will be interested in education, so schools and colleges will offer courses for these people. Because many of the older people work, these courses will be given in the evenings and on weekends.

The needs for housing will be different. It is common now for many people to live in houses that have five or six rooms. This kind of house is good for families with three or four children. But if the population gets older and if families have only one child, large homes will not be necessary. Those people who need only three or four rooms for their homes will live in small apartments. They won't have to take care of a large house.

The change in population will also affect work. If there are fewer and fewer young people and more and more old people, there won't be a big need for cars or for schools. There will be a greater need for buses and hospitals, however.

grandfather /ˈɡrændˌfɑːðə/	n.	祖父,外祖父
grandmother /ˈɡrændˌmʌðə/	n.	祖母,外祖母
grandson /ˈɡrændsʌn/	n.	孙子,外孙
granddaughter /ˈɡrændˌdɔːtə/	n.	孙女,外孙女
common /ˈkɔmən/	adj.	共同的,普通的,一般的
size /saiz/	n.	尺寸,大小
average /ˈævəridʒ/	adj.	平均的
age /eidʒ/	n.	年龄
increase /inˈkriːs/	v.	增加,增长

Unit One Families

/ˈinkriːs/	n.	增加,增长
interest /inˈtrist/	v.	使发生兴趣
/ˈintrist/	n.	兴趣,趣味
education /ˌedjuˈkeiʃən/	n.	教育
college /ˈkɔlidʒ/	n.	学院,高等专科学校
offer /ˈɔfə/	v.	提供,提出
	n.	提供,提出
course /kɔːs/	n.	课程,进程
necessary /ˈnesisəri/	adj.	必需的,必要的
care /kɛə/	n.	小心,注意
	v.	关心,注意
affect /əˈfekt/	v.	影响

Phrases and expressions

be interested in   对……感兴趣
per cent   百分之……

Reading comprehension

Choose the one that best completes each of the following statements according to the text.

(1) There are _____ people in a family now than twenty years ago.
　　A. fewer　　　　　　B. more　　　　　　C. much more

(2) There are _____ old people in the United States now than ten years ago.
　　A. more　　　　　　B. fewer　　　　　　C. much fewer

(3) Schools will also offer courses for _____.
　　A. children　　　　　B. older people　　　C. young people

(4) Courses will be offered to older people _____.
　　A. on their work days　B. in their free time　C. only on weekends

(5) People in small families will live in _____.
　　A. public houses　　　B. small apartments　C. large houses

(6) There will be a greater need for _____.
　　A. teachers　　　　　B. workers　　　　　C. doctors

定语从句(attributive clause)是由关系代词或关系副词引导的从句,其作用是作定语修饰主句的某个名词性成分,相当于形容词,所以又称为形容词性从句。被修饰的词称作定语从句的先行词(antecedent),定语从句一般跟在它所修饰的先行词后面。

限定性定语从句(restrictive attributive clause)多由关系代词和关系副词引导。

一、关系代词

关系代词在句中作主语、宾语或定语。

(1)that 既可代表事物也可代表人,which 代表事物,它们在从句中作主语或宾语,that 在从句中作宾语时常可省略,which 在从句中作宾语也可以省略。例如:

This is the book (which) you want.

(2)如果 which 在从句中作"不及物动词+介词"的介词的宾语,注意介词不要丢掉,而且介词总是放在关系代词 which 的前边,但有的则放在它原来的位置。

(3)代表物时多用 which,但在下列情况中用 that 而不用 which:

①先行词是 anything,everything,nothing,none 等不定代词时;

②先行词由 every,any,all,some,no,little,few,much 等修饰时,这时的 that 常被省略;

③先行词前有序数词或被形容词最高级修饰时;

④先行词中既有人又有物时;

⑤整个句中前面已有 which,who,that 时;

⑥当先行词为物并作表语时;

⑦先行词为 one 时;

⑧先行词同时又被 the only,the very,the same 修饰时。

(4)who 和 whom 引导的从句用来修饰人,分别作从句中的主语和宾语,whom 作宾语时,要注意它可以作动词的宾语也可以作介词的宾语。

(5)whose 是关系代词,修饰名词作定语,相当于所修饰成分的前置所有格,它引导的从句可以修饰人或物,当它引导的从句修饰物体时,可以与 of which 调换,表达的意思一样。

二、关系副词

关系副词在句中作状语。

关系副词=介词+关系代词,如:

why=for which

where=in/at/on/… which(介词同先行词搭配)

when=during/on/in/… which(介词同先行词搭配)

(1)where 是关系副词,用来引导表示地点的定语从句。

(2)when 引导定语从句表示时间。需要注意的是,表示时间"time"一词的定语从句只用 when 引导,有时不用任何关系代词,当然也不用 that 引导。

By the time you arrived in London,we had stayed there for two weeks.

你到达伦敦的时候,我们在那里已经待两个星期了。

I still remember the first time I met her.

我仍然记得我第一次见到她的情景。

Each time he goes on a business trip,he takes a lot of living necessities,such as towels,a soap and a toothbrush.

每一次他去出差,他却带生活必需品,如毛巾、肥皂和牙刷。

(3)当从句的逻辑主语是 some, any, no, somebody, anybody, nobody, something, anything,everything 或 nothing 时,常用 there is 来引导。

There is somebody here who wants to speak to you.

这里有人要和你说话。

Unit One Families

Fun time

Good Boy

Little Robert asked his mother for two cents.

"What did you do with the money I gave you yesterday?"

"I gave it to a poor old woman," he answered.

"You're a good boy," said the mother proudly. "Here are two more cents. But why are you so interested in the old woman?"

"She is the one who sells the candy."

单元复习

I 词汇练习

选择合适的词或词组填入空白处。

course   age   average   example   size   be interested in
ask for   take care of   worry about   as a result of

1. At what _____ do children start school in your country?
2. Our teacher gave us some _____ to show the fact.
3. I have to _____ the boy while his mother is out.
4. The _____ age of the boys in this class is 10.
5. This room is the same _____ as that one.
6. I am sure he will _____ computer science.
7. _____ his health problem, he couldn't finish the job.
8. The school will offer the students some new _____ next year.
9. Don't _____ me. I'll solve the problem soon.
10. I think she will _____ some help.

II 语法练习

1. This is the book _____ about computer science.
   A. who tells   B. which talks   C. that tells   D. that is talking
2. The kind old woman _____ care of my children last year is now in Beijing.
   A. that took   B. who takes   C. which takes   D. which took
3. They live in a house _____ built in 1800.
   A. where was   B. which is   C. that was   D. which are

4. The girls _____ buying books in the bookshop now are students of our school.
   A. who is   B. who are   C. that is   D. which are
5. The desks and chairs _____ repairing are in the meeting room.
   A. which needs   B. all need   C. that need   D. all that needs
6. All those _____ to go camping will get together at the school gate at six tomorrow.
   A. which want   B. who want   C. who wants   D. that wants
7. This is the first old building _____ will be changed soon in the town.
   A. which   B. it   C. that   D. who
8. Is there anything _____ at once?
   A. which has to be done   B. that has to do
   C. that has to be done   D. which have to do

Ⅲ 阅读理解

阅读下面短文,根据短文内容,从短文后面每题所给的选项中选择最佳的一项。

The summer vacation is over. It's true that time always flies fast. During the vacation, the weather was hot and I could not do much work, but I lived happily.

As the afternoon was hot, I did my work in the morning. I used to get up at 6:30 and take a walk in the garden for half an hour. After breakfast, I began reading English and Chinese and did some exercises in maths. Those took me three hours or more. I worked quite hard and made good progress(取得进步).

I spent the afternoon outside. I went to swim and it was funny. I would not go home until it was about five or six o'clock. Sometimes a friend of mine would come to see me and we would spend some hours listening to music.

In this way I spent my vacation happily. And I not only studied well but also became a good swimmer. Now I am in good health and high spirits(精神).

1. What does the text mainly tell us?
   A. How the writer spent his summer holidays.
   B. What the weather was like in that summer.
   C. When the writer got up in the morning.
   D. Where the writer took a walk.
2. How long did it take the writer to do his homework?
   A. Half an hour.   B. Three hours or more.
   C. Only one hour.   D. Two hours and a half.
3. The writer spent most of the afternoon _____.
   A. listening to music   B. visiting his friends
   C. walking in the garden   D. swimming
4. The writer had very good summer holidays because he _____.
   A. worked very hard and made good progress
   B. learned to swim and did his work well

C. got up early and went home late
   D. liked swimming better than studying
5. Which of the following is NOT true?
   A. The writer made progress in his lessons.
   B. The writer took a walk for half an hour before breakfast.
   C. The writer began studying as soon as he got up.
   D. The writer spent more time swimming than listening to music.

Unit Two   Animals

 Warming up

What do you think of these animals?

1. Discussion.

(1) Do you like animals?

(2) Do you want to be an animal keeper?

(3) What animal do you like best?

(4) Why are some wild animals in danger?

(5) What should we do to protect animals?

2. Pair work: Read the following dialogue with your partner.

Boy: Where do you want to go now?

Girl: To see the elephants.

  B: The elephants? Why do you like elephants?

  G: Oh, they're interesting. And they are really intelligent.

  B: Yes, but they are ugly, too.

  G: Oh, Tony! So, where do you want to go?

  B: To see the pandas. They are kind of cute.

  G: Oh, yeah. I love pandas. They're beautiful. But they are also kind of shy. Where are they?

Unit Two Animals

B: They're over there on the left, just across from the koala bears.
G: Then, why don't we see the koala bears first?
B: Sounds great! OK, let's go.

扫一扫跟着练

Colors to Protect Animals

Do you know why different animals or pests have their special colours? Colours in them seem to be used mainly to protect themselves.

Some birds like eating locusts, but birds cannot easily catch them. Why? It is because locusts change their colours together with the change of the colours of crops. When crops are green, locusts look green. But as the harvest time comes, locusts change to the same brown colour as crops have. Some other pests with different colours from plants are easily found and eaten by others. So they have to hide themselves for lives and appear only at night.

If you study the animal life, you'll find the main use of colouring is for self—protection. Bears, lions and other animals move quietly through forests. They cannot be easily seen by hunters. This is because they have the colours much like the trees.

Have you ever found an even stranger act? A kind of fish in the sea can send out a kind of very black liquid when it faces danger. While the liquid spreads over, its enemies cannot find it. And it immediately swims away. So it has lived up to now though it is not strong at all.

扫一扫跟着练

New words

pest /pest/	n.	有害的动物,害虫;有害的植物
locust /ˈləukəst/	n.	蝗虫 a swarm of locusts 一群蝗虫
crop /krɔp/	n.	作物,庄稼
harvest /ˈhɑːvist/	n.	收获;收获季节
liquid /ˈlikwid/	n.	液体
spread /spred/	vt.	撒;散布,传播;普及
hunter /ˈhʌntə/	n.	猎人,猎手

Phrases and expressions

protect oneself	保护自己
self-protection	自我保护
at night	晚上

together with 连同；和
kind of 有些…… 有点……

Reading comprehension

Choose the one that best completes each of the following statements according to the text.

(1) From the passage we can learn that locusts _____.

    A. are small animals

    B. are easily found by birds

    C. are dangerous to their enemies

    D. change their colours to protect themselves

(2) How can pests with different colours from plants keep out of danger?

    A. They run away quickly.

    B. They have the colours much like their enemies.

    C. They hide themselves by day and appear at night.

    D. They have to move quietly.

(3) Bears and lions can keep safe because _____.

    A. they have the colours much like the trees

    B. they move quietly

    C. they like brown and grey colours

    D. they live in forests

(4) Why can the kind of fish live up to now?

    A. Because it is very big and strong.

    B. Because the liquid it sends out can help it escape from its enemies.

    C. Because the liquid it sends out can kill its enemies.

    D. Because it swims faster than any other fish.

(5) Which is the best title for this passage?

    A. The Change of Colours for Animals and Pests.

    B. Colours of Different Animals and Pests.

    C. The Main Use of Colours for Animals and Pests.

    D. Some Animals and Pests.

Grammar

英语中的被动语态

"Some other pests with different colours from plants are easily found and eaten by others."

句子中的 are easily found and eaten by others 属于被动语态。英语中被动语态的基本结构为"be＋过去分词。"

下面是各种时态的被动语态形式及例句。
(1)一般现在时的被动语态构成:is/am/are＋及物动词的过去分词。
Our classroom is cleaned every day.
I am asked to study hard.
Knives are used for cutting things.
(2)一般过去时的被动语态构成:was/were＋及物动词的过去分词。
A new shop was built last year.
Dinosaur eggs were laid long ago.
(3)现在完成时的被动语态构成:has/have＋been＋及物动词的过去分词。
This book has been translated into many languages.
Many man-made satellites have been sent up into space by many countries.
(4)一般将来时的被动语态构成:will＋be＋及物动词的过去分词。
A new hospital will be built in our city.
Many more trees will be planted next year.
(5)含有情态动词的被动语态构成:情态动词＋be＋及物动词的过去分词。
Young trees must be watered often.
Your mistakes should be corrected right now.
The door may be locked inside.
Your homework can be handed in tomorrow.
(6)现在进行时的被动语态构成:am/is/are＋being＋及物动词的过去分词。
My bike is being repaired by Tom now.
Trees are being planted over there by them.
(7)不定式的被动语态:to＋be＋及物动词的过去分词。
There are twenty more trees to be planted.
(8)过去将来时的被动语态:would＋be＋及物动词的过去分词。
He said the work would be finished soon by him.
一般来说,把主动语态改为被动语态非常简单,可以遵循以下几个步骤:
(1)先找出谓语动词。
(2)再找出谓语动词后的宾语。
(3)把宾语用作被动语态中的主语。
(4)注意人称、时态和数的变化。
例如:
①Bruce writes a letter every week.(主动)
　→A letter is written by Bruce every week.(被动)
②Li Lei mended the broken bike this morning.(主动)
　→The broken bike was mended by Li Lei this morning.(被动)
③He has written two novels so far.(主动)
　→Two novels have been written by him so far.(被动)
④They will plant ten trees tomorrow.(主动)
　→Ten trees will be planted by them tomorrow.(被动)

⑤Lucy is writing a letter now.（主动）

→A letter is being written by Lucy now.（被动）

⑥You must lock the door when you leave.（主动）

→The door must be locked when you leave.（被动）

 Fun time

Teacher: Here are two birds, one is a swallow, and the other is a sparrow. Now who can tell us which is which?

Student: I cannot point out but I know the answer.

Teacher: Please tell us.

Student: The swallow is beside the sparrow and the sparrow is beside the swallow.

单元复习

Ⅰ 词汇练习

请选择合适的单词及其正确形式填空。

     pest locust crop harvest liquid spread hunter

1. The severe frost killed off most of the insect _____.

2. They get two _____ of rice a year.

3. Oil, milk and water are all _____.

4. The farmer hired extra workers for the _____.

5. David was a very brave young _____.

6. We can see a swarm of _____.

7. I _____ my arms as far apart as I could.

Ⅱ 语法练习

单项选择题。

1. _____ a new library _____ in our school last year?

 A. Is; built

 B. Was; built

 C. Does; build

 D. Did; build

2. An accident _____ on this road last week.

 A. has been happened

B. was happened

C. is happened

D. happened

3. Cotton _____ in the southeast of China.

   A. is grown   B. are grown
   C. grows   D. grow

4. So far, the moon _____ by man already.

   A. is visited
   B. will be visited
   C. has been visited
   D. was visited

5. A talk on Chinese history _____ in the school hall next week.

   A. is given   B. has been given
   C. will be given   D. gives

6. A lot of things _____ by people to save the little girl now.

   A. are doing   B. are being done
   C. has been done   D. will be done

7. The doctor _____ for yet.

   A. isn't sent
   B. hasn't been sent
   C. won't be sent
   D. wasn't sent

8. —When _____ this kind of computers _____?

   —Last year.

   A. did; use   B. was; used
   C. is; used   D. are; used

9. Who _____ this book _____?

   A. did; written
   B. was; written by
   C. did; written
   D. was; written

10. Mary _____ show me her new dictionary.

    A. has asked to   B. was asked to
    C. is asked   D. asks to

11. A story _____ by Granny yesterday.

    A. was told us   B. was told to us
    C. is told us   D. told us

12. The monkey was seen _____ off the tree.

    A. jump   B. jumps
    C. jumped   D. to jump

• Unit Two   Animals

13. Older people _____ well.
    A. looks after
    B. must be looked after
    C. must look after
    D. looked after

14. Our teacher _____ carefully.
    A. should be listened to
    B. should be listen
    C. be listened
    D. is listened

15. In some part of the world, tea _____ with milk and sugar.
    A. is serving   B. is served
    C. serves   D. served

Ⅲ 阅读理解

阅读下面短文，根据短文内容，从短文后面每题所给的选项中选择最佳的一项。

"Cool" is a word with many meanings. Its old meaning is used to express a temperature that is a little bit cold. As the world has changed, the word has had many different meanings.

"Cool" can be used to express feelings of interest in almost anything.

When you see a famous car in the street, maybe you will say, "It's cool." You may think, "He's so cool," when you see your favourite footballer.

We all maximize(扩大) the meaning of "cool." You can use it instead of many words such as "new" or "surprising." Here's an interesting story we can use to show the way the word is used. A teacher asked her students to write about the waterfall(瀑布) they had visited. On one student's paper was Just the one sentence, "It's so cool." Maybe he thought it was the best way to show what he saw and felt.

But the story also shows a scarcity(缺乏) of words. Without "cool," some people have no words to show the same meaning. So it is quite important to keep some credibility(可信性). Can you think of many other words that make your life as colourful as the word "cool"? I can. And I think they are also very cool.

1. We know that the word "cool" has had _____.
    A. only one meaning
    B. no meanings
    C. many different meanings
    D. the same meaning

2. In the passage, the word "express" means" _____ ".
    A. see   B. show
    C. know   D. feel

3. If you are _____ something, you may say, "It's cool."
   A. interested in	B. angry about
   C. afraid of	D. unhappy with
4. The writer takes an example to show he is _____ the way the word is used.
   A. pleased with	B. strange to
   C. worried about	D. careful with
5. In the passage, the writer suggests(暗示) that the word "cool" _____.
   A. can be used instead of many words
   B. usually means something interesting
   C. can make your life colourful
   D. may not be as cool as it seems

Unit Three Getting Around

How do you get around in a strange place?

1. Discussion.

(1) Do you like travelling?

(2) Have you ever got lost in a new place?

(3) How did you find your way later?

(4) Did you use a map or road signs to find your way?

(5) Have you ever asked for directions?

2. Pair work:Read the following dialogue with your partner.

Mary: Tim, do you take a map with you when you travel?

　Tim: Yes, sometimes, but I find it easier just to ask for directions.

Mary: Do you sometimes get lost?

　Tim: Yes, I lose my way at times, but I always get help from the local people.

Mary: Have you ever been to Japan?

　Tim: No, I haven't. Why do you ask that?

Mary: In Japan there are no street names in many cities. So if you ask a Japanese person for directions they will often say something like "Turn right at the next corner" or "The post office is next to the police station."

Tim: Have you ever been to Los Angeles?
Mary: No. Have you?
Tim: Yes. If you ask people in Los Angeles how far away the post office is, they will say "5 minutes away" or "half an hour away" but not "half a mile" or "20 kilometers."
Mary: Why is that?
Tim: It's because they measure distances in time—how long it takes to get to a place by car.

Text

Dear Jim,

Guess what? I'm now in Chengdu, the capital city of Sichuan Province in southwest China.

At this moment I'm sitting with some of my friends in a teahouse in downtown Chengdu. We are drinking tea and watching Sichuan Opera. It's really wonderful. I am enjoying every minute of my stay here.

Sichuan is fantastic. There are many interesting places to visit. Tomorrow we're going to take a bus to Wolong. There we will see the famous pandas. I like pandas a lot. They are very cute. Every year people from all around the world come to see them.

We will stay in Wolong for two days. Then we will go to Jiuzhaigou. This place is well-known for its beautiful scenery. Some say it is the most beautiful place on Earth.

Of course, I eat famous Sichuan food every day. Most of the dishes are hot and spicy, much hotter than I usually eat, but I still enjoy them.

I like Sichuan a lot and I'm sure you'd like it, too.

Best wishes,
Qiang

 New words

capital /ˈkæpɪtl/	n.	首都;首府;省会
province /ˈprɒvɪns/	n.	省,州
southwest /ˌsaʊθˈwest/	n.	西南,西南方
	adj.	西南的;向西南的;西南部的
teahouse /ˈtiːhaʊs/	n.	茶室;茶馆
colorful /ˈkʌləfəl/	adj.	富有色彩的;鲜艳的

wonderful /ˈwʌndəfəl/	adj.	极好的；精彩的
opera /ˈɔpərə/	n.	歌剧
fantastic /fænˈtæstik/	adj.	【口】极好的，了不起的
panda /ˈpændə/	n.	大熊猫
cute /kjuːt/	adj.	漂亮的，可爱的，聪明的
well-known /ˈwelnəun/	adj.	出名的，知名的
scenery /ˈsiːnəri/	n.	风景，景色
Earth /əːθ/	n.	（常大写）地球
dish /diʃ/	n.	一盘菜；菜肴
spicy /ˈspaisi/	adj.	辛辣的

Phrases and expressions

at this moment	此时，此刻
Sichuan Opera	川剧
be well-known for	以……而闻名

Reading comprehension

Choose the one that best completes each of the following statements according to the text.

(1) Qiang is travelling in Sichuan with his _____.
  A. friends
  B. family
  C. teachers

(2) Sichuan is in the _____ of China.
  A. northeast
  B. southwest
  C. northwest

(3) They drink tea and watch opera _____ Chengdu.
  A. in the centre of
  B. near
  C. outside

(4) Jiuzhaigou is famous for its _____.
  A. scenery
  B. food
  C. tea

(5) Food in Sichuan is _____.
  A. sweet
  B. cold
  C. hot and spicy

Unit Three　Getting Around

 Grammar

1. 形容词的比较级和最高级

(1)在英语中,在表示"比较……"和"最……"时,形容词要用特别的形式,称为"比较级"和"最高级",原来的形容词称为"原级"。

原级	比较级	最高级
strong 强	stronger 较强	strongest 最强

(2)形容词的比较级和最高级的构成方法如下。

①单音节词和少数双音节词以加-er 和-est 的方式构成。

原级	比较级	最高级
young 年轻	younger 较年轻	youngest 最年轻
old 老	older 较老	oldest 最老
clean 干净	cleaner 较干净	cleanest 最干净

在加词尾时要注意下面的各种情况:

情　况	加词尾的方法	例　词
一般情况	直接加词尾	small,smaller,smallest
以 e 结尾的词	加-r,-st	large,larger,largest
以"辅音+y 结尾"的词	变 y 为 i,再加词尾	busy,busier,busiest
以一个"辅音字母"结尾的词	将该辅音字母双写再加词尾	big,bigger,biggest

②不规则形容词的比较级和最高级。

原　级		比较级	最高级
good/well		better	best
bad		worse	worst
many/much		more	most
little		less	least
far		farther	farthest(表示距离)
		further	furthest(表示程度)
old	older	oldest(表示新旧或年龄)	
	elder	eldest(表示兄弟姐妹之间的长幼关系)	

③其他双音节词及多音节词都在前面加 more,most 构成比较级及最高级:

原　级	比较级	最高级
important	more important	most important
difficult	more difficult	most difficult
interesting	more interesting	most interesting
useful	more useful	most useful

2. 现在进行时

例如：At this moment I'm sitting with some of my friends in a teahouse in downtown Chengdu.

(1)构成：主语＋be＋动词的 ing 形式，即：

I＋am＋v. -ing

We(You,They)＋are＋v. -ing

He(She,It)＋is＋v. -ing

(2)定义：现在进行时表示现在或当前一般时间正在进行的动作。

可以表示有计划的未来。有时一般现在时表将来。

(3)现在进行时的基本用法。

① 表示现在(指说话人说话时)正在发生的事情。

We are waiting for you.

②习惯进行：表示长期的或重复性的动作，说话时动作未必正在进行。

Mr. Green is writing another novel.（说话时并未在写，只处于写作的状态。）

Fun time

The Biggest in the World

Peter dozed off while his teacher was talking.

Teacher: Peter! Tell us, what's the biggest in the world?

Peter: Well, well… eyelids…

Teacher: What? Eyelids?

Peter: Yes, sir, because the eyelids cover everything of the world as soon as I shut my eyes.

单元复习

I 词汇练习

选择合适的词或词组填入空白处。

fantastic   teahouse   capital   well-known

cute   scenery   spicy   colorful

1. Chengdu is the _____ city of Sichuan Province in southwest China.

2. My friends and I are drinking tea in a _____.

3. We like watching _____ Sichuan Opera.

Unit Three Getting Around

4. There are many _____ places to visit.

5. Pandas are _____ and interesting.

6. Emeishan is _____ for its culture and history.

7. If you like to eat _____ food, Sichuan is a good choice.

8. Beautiful _____ greets you wherever you look.

Ⅱ 语法练习

1. 用形容词或副词的适当形式填空。

(1) The red pen is short. The yellow one is _____ than the red one, and the blue one is the _____ of the three.

(2) My uncle is old. My father is _____ than my uncle, and my grandfather is the _____ in the big family.

(3) Our classroom is clean. The teachers' office is _____ than our classroom, and the lab is the _____ in our school.

(4) Mary's school bag is cheap. Her sister's bag is _____ than her bag, and my bag is the _____.

(5) This is a very good book. But the book on the table is _____ than this one, and the one over there is the _____.

(6) Tony studies hard. Laura studies _____ than Tony, and Jane studies _____ in our class.

(7) Buses run fast. Trains run _____ than buses, and planes run the _____.

(8) I get up early in the morning. My father gets up _____ than I, and my mother gets up the _____ in my family.

2. 用现在进行时改写下列句子。

(1) My father drinks tea in the teahouse.

_____

(2) Sue watches TV at home.

_____

(3) We play basketball on the playground.

_____

(4) The worker tells us how to use the machine.

_____

(5) The shop assistant helps the customer in the shop.

_____

(6) The tour guide shows the tourist around the city.

_____

(7) The girls swim in the pool.
_____

(8) They run very fast.
_____

Ⅲ 阅读理解

阅读下面短文，根据短文内容，从短文后面每题所给的选项中选择最佳的一项。

When you want to go shopping, decide how much money you can spend for new clothes. Think about the kind of clothes you really need. Then look for those clothes on sale(销售). There are labels(标签) inside all new clothes. The labels tell you how to take care of your clothes. The label for a shirt may tell you to wash it in warm water. A sweater label may tell you to wash by washing in cold water. The label on a coat may say "dry clean only." Washing may ruin(损坏) this coat. If you do as the directions(说明) say on the label, you can keep your clothes looking their best.

Many clothes today must be dry cleaned. Dry cleaning is expensive. When buying new clothes, check(核实) to see if they will need to be dry cleaned. You will save money if you buy clothes that can be washed. You can save money if you buy clothes that are well made. Well-made clothes last longer. They look good even after they have been washed many times. Clothes that cost more money are not always better made. They do not always fit(合身) better. Sometimes less expensive clothes look and fit better than more expensive clothes.

1. If you want to save money, you can buy clothes that _____.

   A. don't fit you

   B. don't last long

   C. need to be dry cleaned

   D. can be washed

2. The labels inside the clothes tell you _____.

   A. how to keep them looking their best

   B. how to save money

   C. whether they fit you or not

   D. where to get them dry cleaned

3. The first thing for you to do before you buy clothes is _____.

   A. to look for well-made clothes

   B. to see how much money you can pay

   C. to know how to wash them

   D. to read the labels inside them

4. We learn from the reading that cheaper clothes _____.

   A. are always worse made

   B. must be dry cleaned

   C. can not be washed

   D. can sometimes fit you better

5. The best title(标题)for the reading should be _____.

   A. Buying Less Expensive Clothes

   B. Taking Enough when Shopping

   C. Being a Clever Clothes Shopper

   D. Choosing the Labels Inside New Clothes

Unit Four Sports

 **Warming up**

Do you often play these sport

1. Discussion.

(1) Do you like sports?

(2) Which sport do you like most?

(3) Do you like to watch football games on TV?

(4) How often do you play football?

(5) What do you know about the history of football?

2. Pair work: Read the following dialogue with your partner.

Woman: Hello, sir. What can I do for you?

    Man: Yes… Er, have you read about The World Cup in today's newspaper, Miss?

Woman: Yes, I have. They're playing the semi-finals, aren't they?

    Man: You bet. Are you interested in football?

Woman: Well. Yes, in a way.

    Man: I am terribly interested in football. In fact, you can call me a football fan. Football is a wonderful game.

Woman: Yes it is. Now, what shoes can I show you, sir?

    Man: In fact, I like all sports and games.

Woman: Oh, yes?

Man: Yes. Football, volleyball, swimming. Can you swim?

Woman: I'm not a good swimmer, but I go swimming sometimes.

Man: And what about running—one man tries to run faster than other men? Do you run?

Woman: No. But I walk quite a lot. Now, what kind of shoes do you want, sir? Perhaps you want some running shoes?

Man: I just want something that makes me feel comfortable when I'm watching TV.

Sports in the World

All over the world people enjoy sports, and nearly everyone is good at some sport or other. Sports help one to keep healthy and happy.

Many people like to watch others play games. They buy tickets or turn on TVs to watch the games. They often get very excited when "their" player or team wins.

Sport change with the seasons. People play different games in winter and summer. Swimming is fun in warm weather, but skating is good in winter.

Games and sports often grow out of people's work and everyday activities. The Arabs use horses or camels in much of their everyday life; they use them in their sports, too. It is the same with people in the northwest of China. Millions of people hunt and fish for a living, but hunting and fishing are very good sport, too. Some sports are so interesting that people everywhere go in for them. Football, for example, is played all over the world. Swimming is popular in all countries near the sea or in those with many rivers. What fun it is to jump into a river or lake, whether in China, Australia or the USA! And think of people in cold countries. What fun it is to skate in Japan, England or Canada!

People from different countries may not be able to understand each other, but after a game together they often become good friends.

New words

sport /spɔːt/	n.	消遣，体育运动（常作 sports）
enjoy /inˈdʒɔi/	v.	欣赏，喜爱，享受，享有
nearly /ˈniəli/	adv.	几乎
healthy /ˈhelθi/	adj.	健康的，健壮的，健全的，卫生的

others /ˈʌðəz/	pron.	其他的人或物，其余的人或物
ticket /ˈtikit/	n.	票，入场券
excited /ikˈsaitid/	adj.	兴奋的，活跃的
season /ˈsiːzn/	n.	季节，时节
weather /ˈweðə/	n.	天气，气象
skating /ˈskeitiŋ/	n.	溜冰，滑冰
everyday /ˈevridei/	adj.	每天的，日常的，普通的
activity /ækˈtiviti/	n.	活动，活动力
hunting /ˈhʌntiŋ/	n.	狩猎，探求
fishing /ˈfiʃiŋ/	n.	钓鱼，渔业
popular /ˈpɔpjulə/	adj.	受欢迎的，通俗的，流行的
skate /skeit/	v.	溜冰
together /təˈgeðə/	adv.	一起地，在一起

Phrases and expressions

all over	浑身，到处
be good at	擅长于……，善于……
some ... or other	某一，某种（表示不肯定）
turn on	打开（电源、气源、水源）
change with	根据……而变化
grow out of	由……而产生
much of ...	……的多数，大部分（修饰不可数名词）
the same with	和……一样
millions of	成百万的
do ... for a living	以做……为生
so ... that ...	如此……以至……
go in for	参加，追求，从事
for example	比如，例如
jump into	跳进
whether ... or ...	是否，是……还是……
think of	想一想，想想，记起，考虑
be able to	能够，有能力做

Proper names

Arab	阿拉伯
Arabs	阿拉伯人

Australia	澳大利亚
USA	美利坚合众国
Canada	加拿大

Reading comprehension

Choose the one that best completes each of the following statements according to the text.

(1) In what ways can sports help people?

  A. To keep themselves physically fit.

  B. To make people feel happy.

  C. Both A and B.

(2) In Canada, the best sport in winter is _____.

  A. hunting and fishing

  B. mountain climbing

  C. skating

(3) Which of the following is true?

  A. People all over the world play football well.

  B. People play football all over the world.

  C. Football is a game played by everyone in the world.

(4) Why is swimming not so popular in Arab as in Australia?

  A. Because they have different life styles.

  B. Because they have different natural surroundings.

  C. Because the people have different interests.

(5) Which of the following sports doesn't come from people's work?

  A. Boxing.

  B. Horse racing.

  C. Fishing and hunting.

名　词

　　名词(Nouns)是词性的一种,也是实词的一种,是表示人、物、事、时、地、情感、概念等实体或抽象事物名称的词。名词可以独立成句。在短语或句子中通常可以用代词来替代。名词可以分为专有名词(Proper Nouns)和普通名词(Common Nouns),专有名词是某个(些)人、地方、机构等专有的名称,如 Beijing, China 等。普通名词是表示一类人或东西名称或是一个抽象概念的名词,如:book, sadness 等。

一、按意义分类

1. 专有名词

表示具体的人、事物、地点、团体或机构的专有名称(第一个字母要大写)。例如:China 中国,Asia 亚洲,Beijing 北京,the People's Republic of China 中华人民共和国。

专有名词如果是含有普通名词的短语,则必须使用定冠词 the。例如:the Great Wall (长城)。

姓氏名如果采用复数形式,则表示该姓氏一家人(复数含义)。例如:the Greens(格林一家人)。

地点、团体或机构的专有名称第一个字母要大写。例如:China 中国,Asia 亚洲。

2. 普通名词

表示某些人、某类事物、某种物质或抽象概念的名称。例如:teacher 老师,tea 茶,reform 改革。

普通名词又可进一步分为以下 4 类:

(1)个体名词(Individual Nouns):表示单个的人和事物。例如:car 汽车,room 房间,fan 风扇,photo 照片。

(2)集体名词(Collective Nouns):表示一群人或一些事物的名称。例如:people 人们,family 家庭,army 军队,government 政府。

(3)物质名词(Material Nouns):表示物质或不具备确定形状和大小的个体的物质。例如:fire 火,steel 钢,air 空气,water 水,milk 牛奶。

(4)抽象名词(Abstract Nouns):表示动作、状态、品质或其他抽象概念。例如:labour 劳动,health 健康,life 生活,friendship 友情,patience 耐力。

二、按是否可数分类

名词又可分为可数名词(Countable Nouns)和不可数名词(Uncountable Nouns)。

1. 不可数名词

不可数名词是指不能以数目来计算,不可以分成个体的概念、状态、品质、感情或表示物质材料的东西。它一般没有复数形式,只有单数形式。它的前面不能用不定冠词 a/an。抽象名词、物质名词和专有名词一般是不可数名词。例如:water 水,rice 米、米饭,youth 青春,paper 纸。

2. 可数名词

可数名词是指能以数目来计算,可以分成个体的人或东西,因此它有复数形式。例如:boys 男孩,holidays 节假日,games 游戏,countries 国家。

三、名词的复数

1. 可数名词的复数

可数名词有单数和复数两种形式。单数变为复数的方法如下。

(1)单数名词词尾加 s。例如:map→maps,boy→boys,horse→horses,table→tables。

(2)以 s,x,sh,ch 结尾的词加 es。例如:class→classes,box→boxes,bus→ buses,dish→dishes。

(3)以 o 结尾的词,变复数时有生命的加 es,无生命的加 s。例如:hero→ heroes,negro→negroes,tomato→tomatoes,potato→potatoes。

(4) 以辅音字母加 y 结尾的名词,变 y 为 i,再加 es。以元音字母加 y 结尾的直接加 s。例如:family→families,city→cities,party→parties。

(5) 以 f 或 fe 结尾的名词,变 f 或 fe 为 v,再加 es。例如:shelf→shelves,wolf→wolves,life→lives,knife→knives。

(6) 以 ce,se,ze,(d)ge 等结尾的词加 s,读|z|。

2. 不可数名词量的表示

(1) 物质名词。

① 当物质名词转化为个体名词时。

Cake is a kind of food.

蛋糕是一种食物。(不可数)

These cakes are sweet.

这些蛋糕很好吃。(可数)

② 当物质名词表示该物质的种类时,名词可数。

This factory produces steel.

这个厂生产钢材。(不可数)

We need various steels.

我们需要各种钢材。(可数)

③ 当物质名词表示份数时,可数。

Our country is famous for tea.

我国因茶叶而闻名。

Two teas, please.

请来两杯茶。

(2) 抽象名词有时也可数。

The four modernizations

四个现代化

物质名词和抽象名词可以借助单位词表一定的数量。

a glass of water 一杯水

a piece of advice 一条建议

四、名词的功能

名词在句中作主语、宾语、介词宾语、宾语补足语、表语和定语。

(1) 主语。

The bag is in the desk.

书包在桌子里边。

(2) 宾语。

I washed my clothes yesterday.

昨天我洗了我的衣服。

(3) 表语。

This is a good book.

这是一本好书。

(4)宾语补足语。

We selected him our <u>monitor</u>.

我们选他为我们的班长。

(5)介词宾语。

Mary lives with her <u>parents</u>.

玛丽和她的父母亲住在一起。

(6)定语。

He is a <u>Party</u> member.

他是一位党员。

Fun time

Boxing and Running

Dan is teaching his son how to box. As he is doing so, he says to his friend, "This is a tough world, so I'm teaching my boy to fight."

Friend: "But suppose he comes up against someone much bigger than he is, who's also been taught how to box."

Dan: "I'm teaching him how to run, too."

单元复习

I 词汇练习

单项选择,选出一个能填入空白处的最佳选项。

1. People _____ the world are waiting for the next Olympic Games.

   A. all of

   B. all over

   C. in

2. Our monitor is very good _____ English. He can easily win the English competition.

   A. in

   B. on

   C. at

Unit Four   Sports

3. Some children are watching games, _____ are playing games on the playground.

   A. others

   B. other

   C. another

4. We are going on diet to _____ fit.

   A. reduce

   B. keep

   C. get

5. There isn't much _____ reading on Saturday evenings.

   A. enjoy

   B. interesting

   C. fun

6. Your new shirt has the same color _____ mine.

   A. as

   B. with

   C. of

7. Peter is planning to _____ business after graduation.

   A. go in for

   B. join

   C. take part in

8. He is practicing very hard _____ he can take part in the sports meet.

   A. and

   B. so

   C. so that

II 语法练习

用所给名词的适当形式或量词填空。

1. They sell _____ (piano) in that shop.

2. Don't eat so many _____ (potato); you will get fat.

3. At the class meeting yesterday we talked about some national _____ (hero) like Nathan Hill and Thomas Jefferson.

4. The _____ (story) told by the old cowboy are all interesting.

5. The Smiths visited at least five _____ (city) in that country.

6. The scientists started their research on physics from different _____ (branch).

7. The host offered me a _____ (milk-shake) and I drank it with joy.

8. Do you want another _____ (bread)?

9. Tom went to the hospital yesterday because there was something wrong with one of his _____ (tooth).

10. There are only two _____ (woman) in the office but I can see ten _____ (man) in it.

11. He isn't wearing any _____ (cloth).

12. Does your mother wear _____ (glass)?

13. I wrote a letter of _____ (thank) to my teacher on _____ (teacher) Day.

14. Don't move the chair. That's _____ (Mary) new chair.

15. All the students visited the _____ (child) Palace on June 1st.

Ⅲ 阅读理解

阅读下面短文,根据短文内容,从短文后面每题所给的选项中选择最佳的一项。

Little Tom down the street calls our dog "the keep dog." Zip is a sheep dog. But when Tom tries to say "sheep," it comes out "keep." And in a way Tom is right. Zip is always bringing things home for us to keep! I'll tell you about some of them. Zip's first present was a shoe. It was made of green silk. We didn't know how Zip found the shoe. But after a moment, Mary, my big sister, told me the shoe had a strange smell. I nodded(点头) and held my nose. "What do you think it is?" "It smells like something for cleaning. I think someone tried to clean a spot(污点) off the shoe. Then he put it at the door to dry." "Along came Zip. And good-bye shoe!" I said. "We should take it back." "We can't," said my sister.

"I know we can't," I said. "We don't know where Zip found it."

"Maybe little Tom is right," Mary said. "Maybe Zip is a keep dog!"

1. The writer and Mary didn't know _____.

   A. what Zip's first present was

   B. how Zip carried its first present home

   C. who owned Zip's first present

   D. what Zip's first present was made of

2. Tom calls Zip "the keep dog" because _____.

   A. the dog likes keeping things

   B. the dog likes playing with shoes

   C. he doesn't know the dog's name

   D. he can't pronounce the word "sheep" well

3. What made the shoe strange was _____.

   A. its colour

   B. its smell

   C. its size

   D. that it was a silk one

4. The word "keep" in the last sentence means "_____".
   A. keeping things for itself
   B. bringing things for others to keep
   C. not letting it run about
   D. taking care of a small child
5. We can know from the reading that the dog _____.
   A. likes to give presents to people
   B. has been kept in at the writer's home
   C. has brought some trouble
   D. likes to be called "the keep dog"

Unit Five   Go Shopping

Warming up

Where do you often go shopping?

1. Discussion.

(1) Do you like shopping?

(2) Where do you usually buy your clothes?

(3) Do you want to be a cashier or a factory worker?

(4) Do you often bargain with the shop assistant when you do shopping?

(5) Do you make a shopping list before you go?

2. Pair work: Read the following dialogue with your partner.

Shop-assistant: Good morning, madam. What can I do for you?

Mrs. Robinson: I'd like some toys and dolls for my children. What do you have to offer, Miss?

Shop-assistant: We've got toy guns, trains, planes, cars, boats, motorbikes, spidermen, supermen, and different types of dolls. We also have a great many toy animals like bears, rabbits, dogs, cats, and deer. Who are you buying them for?

Mrs. Robinson: My son and my daughter. The boy's five and the girl's three. What can you suggest?

Shop-assistant: Normally boys prefer to play with toy guns, model cars and trains. Girls' first choice is usually Barbie dolls. Such pretty dolls are quite attractive to little girls.

Mrs. Robinson: Thank you very much. I don't want my son to play with guns. So a model car for the boy and a Barbie doll for the girl.

Shop-assistant: OK. Just a moment, please.

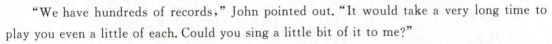

I Suppose You Are New

John works in a shop. The shop sells tape records. One afternoon a middle-aged woman came in, sat on a stool in front of the counter, and smiled at him brightly.

"I want a record, dear," she began. "One I heard on the radio this morning."

"What is the record called?" John asked. The woman shook her head.

"I don't remember. Perhaps if you play me a few records, I shall be able to pick it out."

"We have hundreds of records," John pointed out. "It would take a very long time to play you even a little of each. Could you sing a little bit of it to me?"

The woman shook her head again. "Sorry, I can't sing it at all." Then suddenly her face brightened.

"I've just remembered something," she said. "It comes from a play. The play is about a girl who speaks very badly, if you see what I mean. But after a time she learns to talk well. Something about…"

This was enough for John. "It's from My Fair Lady, I think," he said.

"That's it, dear. If you had thought of it sooner, we wouldn't have wasted so much time," the woman said, "I suppose you are new to the job."

New words

record /ˈrekɔːd/	n.	唱片,录了音的磁带
stool /stuːl/	n.	凳子
counter /ˈkauntə/	n.	柜台
brightly /ˈbraitli/	adv.	愉快地,欢欣地
shake /ʃeik/	v.	(shook, shaken)摇动
pick /pik/	v.	挑,捡
point /pɔint/	v.	指向
brighten /ˈbraitn/	v.	焕发光彩
badly /ˈbædli/	adv.	(worse, worst)不好地,坏地,糟糕地

Phrases and expressions

in front of	在……的前面
pick out	挑出
hundreds of	成百上千
point out	指出
not ... at all	一点也不，完全不
come from	来自，出处

 Reading comprehension

Choose the one that best completes each of the following statements according to the text.

(1) What did the woman want to buy?

    A. A radio.

    B. A record.

    C. A stool.

(2) How did the woman come to know the song?

    A. On the radio.

    B. On TV.

    C. At a concert.

(3) The woman _____ at all.

    A. could sing a little

    B. could sing much

    C. couldn't sing

(4) My Fair Lady is _____.

    A. a play

    B. a cinema

    C. a shop

(5) Was the job new to John?

    A. We don't know.

    B. Yes.

    C. No.

 Grammar

一般现在时

    一般现在时用来表示一般时间发生的动作或行为，并不着眼于现在。它用来表示所有时候的动作和行为，或是普遍真理，而动作是否发生在说话时并不重要。

Nurses look after patients in hospitals.

医院里由护士照看病人。

I usually go away at weekends.

我通常在周末出去。

The earth goes round the sun.

地球绕着太阳转。

1. 基本结构

肯定式	疑问式	否定式	否定疑问式
I work.	Do you work?	I do not work.	Don't you work?
You work.	Do you work?	You do not work.	Don't you work?
We work.	Do you work?	We do not work.	Don't you work?
They work.	Do they work?	They do not work.	Don't they work?
He(She,It) works.	Does he(she,it) work?	He(She,It) does not work.	Doesn't he(she it) work?

注：用 he/she/it 作主语时，不要忘了动词原形后加"s"。

2. 动词第三人称单数一般现在时的变化规律

情 况	构成方法	读 音	例 词
一般情况	加-s	清辅音后读/s/ 浊辅音和元音后读/z/	swim—swims help—helps like—likes
以 o 结尾的词	加-s 或-es	读/z/	goes,does
以 s,sh,ch,x 等结尾的词加-es	读/iz/	watches	
以辅音字母＋y 结尾的词	变 y 为 i 再加 es	读/z/	study—studies
Have	变 have 为 has	读/hæz/	have—has

3. 用法

(1)表示经常的或习惯性的动作,常与表示频率的时间状语连用,如：

always, usually, regularly, every morning/night/evening/day/week/year, often, sometimes, occasionally, from time to time, twice a week, rarely, seldom, once a month, hardly

I leave home for school at 7:00 every morning.

(2)表示主语具备的性格、能力、特征和状态。

I don't want so much.

Xiaoqiang writes good English but does not speak well.

(3)表示客观事实和普遍真理。

Shanghai lies in the east of China.

(4)表示格言或警句。

Pride goes before a fall. 骄者必败。

Big Head

"All the kids make fun of me," the boy cried to his mother. "They say I have a big head."

"Don't listen to them," his mother comforted him. "You have a beautiful head. Now stop crying and go to the store for ten pounds of potatoes."

"Where's the shopping bag?"

"I haven't got one. Use your hat."

单元复习

I 词汇练习

选择合适的词或词组并以适当的形式填入空白处。

middle-aged   point out   smile at   think of   pick out
waste   a few   hundreds of   remember   shake

1. Can you _____ the mistakes in this passage?
2. I can't _____ his name at the moment.
3. He _____ the child and said "Hello."
4. You should study hard and _____ no time at school.
5. She finally _____ the address.
6. Are your friends here? Yes, _____ are here.
7. The floor _____ when he walked across the room.
8. Who's that _____ man over there?
9. We _____ the best piece of silk for that customer.
10. _____ people attended the meeting.

II 语法练习

1. 用不定冠词 a/an 填空。

(1) I am _____ engineer.

(2) She is _____ English teacher.

(3) My father is not _____ cook. He is _____ driver.

(4) Are you _____ hairdresser or _____ nurse?
(5) She is _____ secretary. She helps her boss by finding information.

2. 用所给动词的适当形式填空。
(1) Mary usually _____ (get) up at 6:30 in the morning.
(2) The tour guide _____ (show) the visitors around the park.
(3) Henry _____ (go) to school very early every day.
(4) The secretary often _____ (write) reports for the boss.
(5) I _____ (be) glad to hear from my good friend, Jane.
(6) This _____ (be) an email from his mother in America.
(7) Every morning the shop assistants _____ (greet) visitors at the gate.
(8) They usually _____ (watch) TV in the evening. Only the grandfather _____ (listen) to the radio.

Ⅲ 阅读理解

阅读下面短文,根据短文内容,从短文后面每题所给的选项中选择最佳的一项。

Tom didn't live too far from school. So he went there and back on foot every day. On his way to school he passed(路过) a wet playground when it rained. One day the boy came home very wet. His mother became angry and said, "Don't play in the water on your way home or to school." The next day he came home very wet again. His mother became even angrier. "I'll tell your father if you come home wet again." she said, "Then he'll punish(惩罚) you." The next day the young boy was dry when he came home from school. "You were a good boy today," his mother said, "You didn't play in the water." "No," he answered sadly, "There were so many older boys in the water when I got there this afternoon that there wasn't any room for me at all."

1. Tom _____.
   A. lived too far away from school
   B. didn't come back home every day
   C. went to school with his mother
   D. walked to school

2. There was a _____ on his way to school.
   A. bridge   B. lake
   C. wet ground   D. playground

3. Tom's mother got angry because _____.
   A. Tom was all wet
   B. Tom was dry
   C. Tom was punished
   D. it rained

4. Which of the following is true?
   A. Tom played in the water three times.

B. Tom didn't play in the water the third day.
   C. Many older boys played in the water with Tom the third day.
   D. Tom became a good boy the third day.
5. From the story we know that _____.
   A. Tom didn't want to play in the water later
   B. Tom's father punished him
   C. Tom liked to play in the water
   D. Tom was afraid of his parents

Unit Six   Holidays

Warming up

What do you know about these holidays?

1. Discussion.

(1) Do you send Christmas cards to your friends?

(2) Do you play tricks on others on April Fools' Day?

(3) Is Thanksgiving Day celebrated by the English?

(4) Have you heard of Valentine's Day?

(5) Have you heard of Halloween?

2. Pair work: Read the following dialogue with your partner.

Jeniffer: Mike, it's November already. Before you know it, Thanksgiving will be here.

Mike: Yes, you're right, Jeniffer. It's about time that we decided what we are going to do this year. Do you feel up to inviting the whole family here?

Jeniffer: Sure. After all, it's our turn. We did go to your brother's last year.

Mike: Well, if you're willing to have it at our place, it's fine with me. How about asking your sister to come, too?

Jeniffer: I don't know if she will come. You know, it's such a long trip. But I'll call her and see if she can come.

Mike: Good. What about the turkey?

Jeniffer: That's no problem. It's quite easy to get turkeys at this time of year.

Mike: Look, I'll be glad to help you out with the shopping if you make me a list.

Text

Valentine's Day

On February 14 each year, lovers across the world exchange candy, flowers, and gifts, all in the name of St. Valentine. But who is this mysterious saint and why do we celebrate this holiday?

Valentine was a priest in the third century in Rome. At that time, Rome was ruled by an emperor named Claudius II. He wanted to have a big army to defend his empire. He expected men to join the army, but many men just did not want to fight in wars because they refused to leave their families. This made Claudius extremely angry. He thought that if men were not married, they would not mind joining the army. So Claudius decided not to allow any more marriages.

As a kind-hearted priest, Valentine thought the new law was cruel, so he decided not to support that law! He continued to perform marriages for young lovers in secret. When Valentine's actions were discovered, Claudius had him arrested and put to prison.

Hearing about Valentine's arrest, many young people went to the prison to visit him. One of them was the daughter of the prison guard, who allowed her to visit Valentine in the cell. Sometimes they would sit and talk for hours. She helped him to keep his spirits up. She agreed that Valentine did the right thing. On the day Valentine was going to be put to death, he left her a little note thanking her for her friendship and loyalty. He signed it, "Love from your Valentine." That note started the custom of exchanging love messages on Valentine's Day. It was written on February 14, 269 A.D.

Now, every year on this day, people remember him. But most importantly, they think about love and friendship. And when they think of Emperor Claudius who tried to stand in the way of love, they laugh—because they know that love can't be forbidden!

New words

across	/əˈkrɒs/	prep.	遍及，遍布
exchange	/iksˈtʃeindʒ/	vt.	交换，交流
candy	/ˈkændi/	n.	糖果
mysterious	/misˈtiəriəs/	adj.	神秘的

Unit Six   Holidays

saint /seint/	n.	圣人,圣徒
celebrate /ˈselibreit/	v.	庆祝
priest /priːst/	n.	牧师
rule /ruːl/	vt.	统治
emperor /ˈempərə/	n.	皇帝
defend /diˈfend/	vt.	保卫,保护;为……辩护
empire /ˈempaiə/	n.	帝国
join /dʒɔin/	vt.	加入,参加
extremely /iksˈtriːmli/	adv.	极其
allow /əˈlau/	vt.	允许
marriage /ˈmæridʒ/	n.	婚姻
kind—hearted /kaindˈhaːtid/		好心肠的
law /lɔː/	n.	法律
support /səˈpɔːt/	vt.	支持;赡养
perform /pəˈfɔːm/	vt.	主持,举办;履行
secret /ˈsiːkrit/	n.	秘密,私下
	adj.	秘密的
arrest /əˈrest/	vt. & n.	逮捕
prison /ˈprizn/	n.	监狱
guard /gaːd/	n.	卫兵,守卫
cell /sel/	n.	单间牢房
spirit /ˈspirit/	n.	精神
death /deθ/	n.	死亡
loyalty /ˈlɔiəlti/	adj.	忠诚,忠实
sign /sain/	vt.	署名于,在……上面签名
remember /riˈmembə/	v.	怀念,纪念
forbid /fəˈbid/	vt.	禁止(过去式 forbade,过去分词 forbidden)

 ## Phrases and expressions

in the name of	以……的名义
at that time	当时,在那时
not … any more	再也不,不再
in secret	秘密地,私下地
put … to prison	把……投入监狱
hear about	听说

43

keep one's spirits up　　　　保持精神高昂
put...to death　　　　　　　处死
most importantly　　　　　　最重要的是
stand in the way of　　　　　妨碍,阻止

Proper names

Valentine's Day /ˈvæləntainz dei/　　　瓦伦丁节,情人节
St. Valentine /seint ˈvæləntain/　　　 圣瓦伦丁
Rome /rəum/　　　　　　　　　　　　罗马
Claudius Ⅱ /ˈkldjəsðəˈsekənd/　　　　克劳迪乌斯二世
A. D. (Anno Domini 的缩写)/ˈei di/　　公元

Reading comprehension

Choose the one that best completes each of the following statements according to the text.

(1) Lovers across the world celebrate their holiday to _____.

　　A. remember St. Valentine

　　B. exchange expensive gifts

　　C. criticize a cruel Roman emperor

(2) Men refused to join the army because _____.

　　A. Rome already had a large army to defend its empire

　　B. they had too much work to do during the day

　　C. they did not want to leave their wives and children

(3) Emperor Claudius law to forbid marriage was _____.

　　A. meaningful

　　B. clever

　　C. foolish

(4) Priest Valentine continued to perform marriages for young lovers because he _____.

　　A. was cruel

　　B. was kind-hearted

　　C. wanted to make money

(5) Why do people laugh at Emperor Claudius' law?

　　A. Because love can not be forbidden.

　　B. Because they have Valentine's help.

　　C. Because lovers are stronger than law.

Unit Six　Holidays

 Grammar

"have＋宾语＋过去分词"结构

1. "have＋宾语＋过去分词"结构表示"请（让、使、叫）某人做某事"

I had my car cleaned.

我叫人擦了车子。（是别人擦的，而不是自己擦的）

Why don't you have your TV set repaired ?

你为什么不让人把电视机修理一下呢？（雇人修理）

He had his hair cut.

他理了发。（是别人替他理）

He had cut his hair.（过去完成时）

他自己理了发。（在说话之前的某个时刻他自己给自己理了发）

2. "have＋宾语＋过去分词"结构在口语中可以用来代替常表示意外或不幸遭遇的被动态动词

He has his fruit stolen before he had a chance to pick it.

他树上的果子还没来得及摘就被人偷掉了。

He had two of his teeth knocked out in the fight.

他在打架中被人打掉了两颗牙齿。

The houses had their roofs ripped off by the gale.

房子被狂风掀掉了屋顶。

The cat got her tail singed through sitting too near the fire.

猫坐得太靠近炉火，尾巴上的毛被烤焦了。

3. have 的句型转换

(1) have 可用于否定句和疑问句，都由助动词构成。

—Do you have your windows cleaned every month ?

你每个月都让人擦窗户吗？

—I don't have them cleaned；I clean them myself.

我不让别人擦；我自己擦。

(2) have 可用于进行时形式。

While I was having my hair done, the police towed away my car.

当我在让人给我做头发时，警察把我的汽车拖走了。

I can't ask you to dinner this week as I am having my house painted at the moment.

我这星期不能请你吃饭了，因为我正在让人粉刷房子。

(3) 在非正式英语中，have 经常由 get 来代替。

She got him to dig away the tree.

她让他把树挖走。

45

I Just had a Dream About It

A young woman was taking an afternoon nap. After she woke up, she told her husband, "I just dreamed that you gave me a pearl necklace for Valentine's Day. What do you think it means?"

"You'll know tonight," he said.

That evening, the man came home with a small package and gave it to his wife. Delighted, she opened it—only to find a book entitled The Meaning of Dreams.

单元复习

I 词汇练习

单项选择，选出一个能填入空白处的最佳选项。

1. He _____ the black jacket for a blue one.

   A. brought

   B. exchanged

   C. changed

2. Tom has been arrested _____ drunk driving again.

   A. for

   B. with

   C. of

3. I'm going to ask _____ of you to speak for three minutes.

   A. everything

   B. every

   C. each

4. She was angry at Lennie for _____ her dreams coming true.

   A. standing in the way of

   B. keeping up

   C. putting to prison

5. The peace talk was held _____.

   A. in prison

Unit Six   Holidays

B. in secret

C. in charge

6. Harry _____ his thirtieth birthday with a meal in an expensive restaurant.

　　A. celebrated

　　B. took place

　　C. defended

7. During the war years, the song helped keep our _____ up and we need it now.

　　A. moods

　　B. tempers

　　C. spirits

8. Tom was _____ for attacking a man.

　　A. heard about

　　B. put to prison

　　C. put in charge

9. During the war, a great many young men lost their lives in _____ their homeland.

　　A. defending

　　B. expecting

　　C. ruling

10. The child was _____ to leave the house as a punishment.

　　A. remembered

　　B. forbidden

　　C. allowed

Ⅱ 语法练习

把下列括号内的动词以适当的形式填入空白处。

1. As a kind-hearted priest, Valentine thought the new law was cruel, so he decided _____ (not support) that law.

2. He continued _____ (perform) marriages for young lovers in secret.

3. One of them was the daughter of the prison guard, who allowed her _____ (visit) Valentine in the cell.

4. She helped him _____ (keep) his spirits up.

5. On the day Valentine was going _____ (be) put to death, he left her a little note thanking her friendship and loyalty.

6. When they think of Emperor Claudius who tried _____ (stand) in the way of love, they laugh—because they know that love can't be forbidden!

7. I feel that he will be a good NBA player, and he has a chance _____ (be) a great player.

8. He promised _____ (never make) the same mistake again.

Ⅲ 阅读理解

阅读下面短文,根据短文内容,从短文后面每题所给的选项中选择最佳的一项。

Bob always took the newspaper to Grandpa White's home last before going home. Grandpa White's was at the end of the road. Bob liked Grandpa White. He was often waiting for him near the front gate with sweets or a nice cake. Besides, he often asked Bob about things he was doing—about what he was going to do for the summer and what he liked to do. The thing that Bob didn't like about Grandpa was his never-ending stories about his boyhood(童年) in California. Bob never asked to hear about Grandpa's boyhood, but he couldn't get away.

After Grandpa's wife died in October, Bob could see that Grandpa was lonelier than ever. He would often join Bob halfway along the road and walk along with him as he gave out the papers. Grandpa seemed to have all day, and Bob often was late getting his papers to his customers(订报者). Bob didn't want to complain(抱怨), but the customers were unhappy.

1. When he took the newspaper to Grandpa White, Bob would often receive _____.

   A. old newspapers

   B. sweets or a cake

   C. some money

   D. a paper with questions for him to answer

2. Which do you think is true?

   A. Bob lived with Grandpa.

   B. Grandpa had many stories about his boyhood

   C. Grandpa didn't like to read newspapers.

   D. Bob took the newspaper to Grandpa first.

3. Bob could do nothing when _____.

   A. the customers got their newspapers late

   B. Grandpa began to tell him about his boyhood

   C. he saw Grandpa feeling lonely

   D. Grandpa asked him about the things he was doing

4. The reading mainly(主要) tells us that _____.

   A. Bob was still a child

   B. Grandpa liked to tell stories

   C. the customers sometimes got angry

   D. lonely people need other people

5. The sentence "Grandpa seemed to have all day" means "_____".
   A. Grandpa always seemed to like daytime
   B. Grandpa liked telling stories to Bob all day
   C. Grandpa liked to stay with Bob all the time
   D. Grandpa seemed to be lonely all day

Unit Seven   Water

Warming up

How much do you know about

1. Discussion.

(1) How much water is there in the world?

(2) Where is the water we use from?

(3) How does the water come into plants?

(4) Where does the water below the surface of the earth come from?

(5) Do you think we will use up all the water in the world one day?

2. Pair work: Read the following dialogue with your partner.

Mother: Oh, my baby, look at your hands! So muddy! Do wash your hands with water.

　　Boy: OK, Mum, but I don't know where the water is.

Mother: Oh, no, why, you are so naughty. Just go to the kitchen or the washroom.

　　Boy: Mum, I have cleaned my hands already.

Mother: All right. You should wash your hands once they are dirty from now on.

　　Boy: I've got it! I just remember water to remind myself.

Mother: It sounds good! … What's the sound?

　　Boy: Sound? Sorry, Mum, I do not know what you mean.

Mother: Just like raining. Oh, have you turned off the water faucet?

• Unit Seven   Water

Boy: What a pity! It is my fault since I forgot to shut the water.

Mother: Never waste water, you know water is the essence of life. Although nearly 75% of the earth's surface is covered with water, about 97% of this huge amount is sea water, or salt water. Man can only drink and use the other 3%—the fresh water that comes from rivers, lakes and others.

Boy: I will save the water in the future.

Mother: You know when you are saving the water, you are becoming rich, since everyone should form the habit of thriftiness.

Boy: Habit is the second nature. I will correct bad habits. Water is simple but invaluable. Thank you, Mum.

A Thirsty World

The world is not only hungry, but it is also thirsty for water. This may seem strange to you, since nearly 75 percent of the earth's surface is covered with water. But about 97 percent of this huge amount is seawater, or salt water. Man can only drink and use the other 3 percent—the fresh water from rivers, lakes, underground and other sources. And we cannot even use all of that, because some of it is in the form of icebergs and glaciers. Even worse, some of it has been polluted.

However, as things stand today, this small amount of fresh water is still enough for us. But our need for water is increasing rapidly—almost day by day. Only if we take steps to deal with this problem now can we avoid a severe worldwide water shortage later on.

We all have to learn how to stop wasting our precious water. One of the first steps is to develop ways of reusing it.

Today, in most large cities, water is used only once and then discharged into a sewer system. From there it eventually returns to the sea or runs into underground storage tanks. But it is possible to pipe used water to a purifying plant. There it can be filtered and treated with chemicals so that it can be used again, just as if it were fresh from a spring.

But even if every large city purified and reused its water, we still would not have enough. All we'd have to do to make use of the vast reserves of seawater in the world is to remove the salt. This process is called desalinization, and it is already in use in many parts of the world.

If we take these steps we'll be in no danger of drying up!

51

New words

thirsty /ˈθɜːsti/	adj.	干渴的；干旱的
salt /sɔːlt/	adj.	含盐的
	n.	盐
underground /ˈʌndəɡraʊnd/	n.	地面下层
form /fɔːm/	n.	形式
iceberg /ˈaɪsbɜːɡ/	n.	冰山；流冰
glacier /ˈɡlæsjə/	n.	冰河，冰川
pollute /pəˈluːt/	vt.	弄脏，污染
rapidly /ˈræpɪdli/	adv.	快地，迅速地
avoid /əˈvɔɪd/	vt.	避免；防止
severe /sɪˈvɪə/	adj.	严肃的，严重的
worldwide /ˈwɜːldwaɪd/	adj.	世界范围的
shortage /ˈʃɔːtɪdʒ/	n.	不足，缺乏
waste /weɪst/	vt.	浪费；缺少
reuse /ˌriːˈjuːz/	vt.	再使用
discharge /dɪsˈtʃɑːdʒ/	vt.	卸（货）；排出（液体、气体等）
sewer /ˈsjuə/	n.	阴沟，下水道
storage /ˈstɔːrɪdʒ/	n.	储藏；储藏库
storage tank /ˈstɔːrɪdʒ tæŋk/		储水池
purify /ˈpjʊərɪfaɪ/	vt.	使纯净，使净化
filter /ˈfɪltə/	vt.	过滤
treat /triːt/	vt.	对待；处理
spring /sprɪŋ/	n.	泉，源泉
vast /vɑːst/	adj.	巨大的；大量的
reserve /rɪˈzɜːv/	n.	储备（物）；储藏量
desalination /ˌdiːsælɪˈneɪʃn/	n.	脱盐

Phrases and expressions

be thirsty for	渴望（得到）……
in the form of	以……形式；呈……状态
as things stand	就目前情况来看
day by day	天天，日复一日
only if	只有
take steps	采取措施
deal with	处理；涉及
later on	后来，以后

• Unit Seven   Water

run into	跑进；注入，流入
as if	好像
make use of	利用
in use	正在使用中
be in danger of	处于……危险之中
dry up	（使）干涸

Reading comprehension

Choose the one that best completes each of the following statements according to the text.

(1) What is meant by the phrase "the world" in the first line?

    A. It means people in general.

    B. It means all living things.

    C. It means the earth.

(2) How much of the earth's water can man really use?

    A. Nearly 75 percent of it.

    B. Exactly 3 percent of it.

    C. Less than 3 percent of it.

(3) How can we avoid a worldwide water shortage in the future?

    A. We can invent ways of increasing rainfall.

    B. We can develop ways of reusing water.

    C. We may use less water.

(4) Which of the following statements is true?

    A. Water can only be used once.

    B. Used water can be recycled.

    C. Recycled water is unfit for drinking.

(5) We can't use all of the fresh water because _____.

    A. it is too expensive

    B. it is salty and dirty

    C. some of it is in the form of icebergs and glaciers, and some of it has been polluted

Grammar

数　词

一、数词的定义

表示"多少"和"第几"的词，叫数词。其用法相当于名词或者形容词。数词分为基数词和序数词两种。表示数目（多少）的词是基数词，表示数目顺序（第几）的词用序数词。

二、基数词的表示法

(1)以下是最基本的基数词。

one(1)	two(2)	three(3)	four(4)
five(5)	six(6)	seven(7)	eight(8)
nine(9)	ten(10)	eleven(11)	twelve(12)
thirteen(13)	fourteen(14)	fifteen(15)	sixteen(16)
seventeen(17)	eighteen(18)	nineteen(19)	twenty(20)
thirty(30)	forty(40)	fifty(50)	sixty(60)
seventy(70)	eighty(80)	ninety(90)	a hundred(100)
a thousand(1 000 一千)	a million(100 000 一百万)	a billion(十亿)	

(2)21～99 的表示法。先说"几十",再说"几",中间加连字符。

21 twenty-one

36 thirty-six

45 forty-five

99 ninety-nine

(3)101～999 的表示法。先说"几百",后接 and,再加末尾两位数(或末位数)。

101 one hundred and one

530 five hundred and thirty

789 seventy hundred and eighty-nine

902 nine hundred and two

(4)1 000 以上的基数词的表示法。先从后向前数,每三位数加一个逗号(即以此把数目分为若干段)。第一个逗号前的数为 thousand(千),第二个逗号前的数为 million(百万),第三个逗号前的数为 billion(十亿),然后一段一段地数。

9,883　nine thousand,eight hundred and eighty-three

265,468　two hundred and sixty-five thousand,four hundred and sixty-eight

60,263,150　sixty million,two hundred and sixty-three thousand,one hundred and fifty

三、基数词的用法

(1)"数词＋名词＋形容词"组成复合形容词。

只能做表语,表示一种度量,如长度、高度、宽度、面积的多少等。

The mountain is nearly 300 meters high.

(2)表示编号。编号的事物可用基数词。

①单纯的编号,可在基数词前加 number,简写为 No.。如:No.2 第二。

②序号与事物名词连用,用"a/the＋number/No.＋基数词＋名词"。如:

a No. 3 bus 一辆三路公共汽车;the No. 3 bus 那辆三路公共汽车

Today we are going to study Lesson Five. 今天我们要学习第五课。

(3)表示岁月、年代、日期。

①"In＋the＋基数词复数"表示……年代。

This took place in the 1950s.

这事发生在20世纪50年代。
②表示"年,月,日"。
1949 年读作 nineteen forty-nine
6 月 23 日读作 June (the)twenty-third 或 the twenty-third of June
(4)表示钟点。
半小时用 half,一刻钟用 a quarter,半小时以内用 past,超过半小时用 to。
09:15 nine fifteen 或 a quarter past/after nine
02:30 two thirty 或 half past/after two
(5)用于加减乘除。
One plus two is three. 一加二等于三。
Eight minus four is four. 八减四等于四。
Two times two is four. 二乘二等于四。
Ten divided by two is five. 十除以二等于五。
(6)表示百分数。通常用基数词+percent+of 的形式。
注意:
①要用基数词。
②percent 必须用单数形式。
③percent 前没有 the。
④必须带有 of。
Thirty percent of them is water. 它们当中有30%的水。
Eighty percent of what he said is true. 他的话有80%是真实的。
(7)表示分数。
分子用基数词,分母用序数词;除了分子为 1 的情况下,序数词要用复数形式。
One-fifth of the books are mine. 五分之一的书是我的。
Three-tenths of water is disappeared. 十分之三的水不见了。
(8)表示小数。
5.5   five point five
12.135   twelve point one three five

四、序数词的表示法

(1)以下是最基本的序数词。

first(第1)	second(第2)	third(第3)	fourth(第4)
fifth(第5)	Sixth(第6)	seventh(第7)	eighth(第8)
ninth(第9)	Tenth(第10)	eleventh(第11)	twelfth(第12)
thirteenth(第13)	fourteenth(第14)	fifteenth(第15)	sixteenth(第16)
seventeenth(第17)	eighteenth(第18)	nineteenth(第19)	twentieth(第20)
thirtieth(第30)	fortieth(第40)	fiftieth(第50)	sixtieth(第60)
seventieth(第70)	eightieth(第80)	ninetieth(第90)	

(2)非整十的多位数,将个位数变成序数词即可。

第 21　　　　　　　　twenty-first
第 36　　　　　　　　thirty-sixth
第 99　　　　　　　　ninety-ninth
第 365　　　　　　　three hundred and sixty-fifth

(3)hundred,thousand,million 等序数词形式为 hundredth,thousandth,millionth 等。

第 500　　five hundredth(500th)
第 10 000　　ten thousandth(10,000th)

注意:这类词前面用数字"一"时,这个"一"只用 one,不用 a。

one hundredth　　第 100(不说 a hundredth)

五、序数词的用法

序数词主要用作定语、表语。前面要加定冠词 the。

Is this your first visit to Beijing?
这是你第一次访问北京吗?
The fifth lesson is very easy to learn.
第五课很好学。
You are the first one I believe.
你是我最相信的人。
The fist round of voting hasn't finished.
第一轮投票还没有结束。

 Fun time

Father and Son

A boy is sent to bed by his father. Five minutes later, the boy said, "Dad…"
"What?"
"I'm thirsty. Can you bring me some water?"
"No. Lights out,"Dad replied.
A little later, the boy asked, "Dad…"
"WHAT?"
"I'm thirsty…Can I have some water?"
"I said NO! If you ask again, I'll hit(揍)you!"
Then…"Dad…"
"WHAT?"
"When you come here to hit me, can you bring me some water?"

Unit Seven Water

单元复习

I 词汇练习

单项选择，选出一个能填入空白处的最佳选项。

1. The trees _____ fruit.
   A. grow
   B. are covered with
   C. take

2. _____ money is spend on scientific research every year.
   A. Many
   B. A little
   C. A huge amount of

3. _____ there were difficulties, the Curies went on with their scientific experiment.
   A. Even if   B. only if   C. As if

4. The teacher is taking good care of the students _____ they were her own children.
   A. as far as   B. as if   C. as well as

5. The small stream _____ the big river.
   A. runs out of   B. run away from C. runs into

6. Were you able to _____ those reference books?
   A. make up   B. make for   C. make use of

7. I don't know how to _____ these naughty children.
   A. deal with   B. put up with   C. interfere with

8. My cousin is getting stronger _____.
   A. everyday   B. every day   C. day by day

9. Is this typewriter _____?
   A. in trouble   B. in use   C. in danger

10. The population of the town _____ by five percent last year.
    A. increased   B. expanded   C. extended

II 语法练习

单项选择。

1. The teacher asked each student to write an _____ composition in Chinese.
   A. eight-hundred-words   B. eight-hundreds-word
   C. eight-hundreds-words   D. eight-hundred-word

57

2. The number of the students in our school adds up to _____.

   A. two thousand and three hundred and thirty-two

   B. two thousand three hundred and thirty-two

   C. two thousand three hundred thirty-two

   D. two thousand and three hundred thirty-two

3. It is reported that _____ of the population in these areas are farmers.

   A. two three   B. two third

   C. two thirds   D. second third

4. My uncle began to teach himself German when he was already in his _____.

   A. forties   B. forty

   C. fortieth   D. forty's

5. —When were you born?

   —I was born _____.

   A. in October eight, nineteen eighty-five

   B. in October eighth, nineteen eighty-five

   C. on October eighth, nineteen eighty-five

   D. on October eight, nineteen eight-fifth

6. Every day _____ come to visit this beautiful village.

   A. hundred of people   B. hundreds people

   C. two hundred of people   D. hundreds of people

7. —How many people do you need to clean the windows?

   —We need _____ girls.

   A. three another   B. other three

   C. another three   D. more three

8. He went to live in the countryside in _____ and learned a lot from the peasants.

   A. the 1980's   B. the 1980

   C. 1980s   D. 1980's

9. —How long will it take us to get to No. 1 Middle School?

   —I think it's only _____ walk.

   A. five minute   B. a five-minute

   C. five minutes   D. a five-minutes

10. We worked for _____ hours and got the task finished in time.

    A. a half and three   B. three and half

    C. three and half an   D. three and a half

Ⅲ 阅读理解

阅读下面短文，根据短文内容，从短文后面每题所给的选项中选择最佳的一项。

One day Mr. and Mrs. White go shopping by car. They stop their car near a store. They buy a lot of things and they want to put the things in the car. But Mr. White can't open the

• Unit Seven Water

door of the car, so they ask a policeman to help them. The policeman is very friendly to help them. Just then a man comes up and shouts, "What are you doing with my car?"

　　Mr. and Mrs. White take a look at the car's number and they are frozen there. It isn't their car.

1. Mr. and Mrs. White drive for _____.
   A. fishing
   B. shopping
   C. business
2. They stop their car _____.
   A. at the parking spot
   B. near the sea
   C. near the store
3. They want to put the things _____.
   A. in a big bag
   B. in their car
   C. in other's car
4. Mr. White can't open the car, so _____.
   A. they walk home
   B. they ask a policeman to help
   C. they call a taxi

Unit Eight   Science

 Warming up

How much do you know about them?

1. Discussion.

(1) Some of the scientific and technological discoveries have changed or will change the way people live. Please think:
- In what way do these discoveries change our lives for the better?
- In what way do these discoveries change our lives for the worse?

(2) Talk about popular science and modern technology with your partner.

2. Pair work: Read the following dialogue with your partner.

Man: Our world is becoming very crowded. Some people don't have enough food. The problem is getting worse every year.

Woman: What can we do about that?

Man: I think population growth is a big problem. The world's population is growing too fast, especially in poor countries. In my opinion, every country should make a law saying that a couple can have only one child or two at most.

Woman: I disagree. The number of people in the world is not so important. I think there is a better answer. We should learn better ways to grow food crops. Then there will be enough food for everyone.

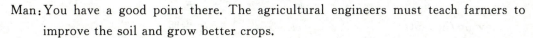

Man: You have a good point there. The agricultural engineers must teach farmers to improve the soil and grow better crops.
Woman: I quite agree with you. I think we also need to use farmland properly. In my opinion, the government should spend more money on agricultural education.
Man: That's right. We must teach the farmers new technology and advanced skills, such as how to use computers in their crop production, and also how to use computers to raise healthier animals.
Woman: Yeah, robots could help to do that.
Man: You are right. And I'm sure we will have other ways to improve food production.

Weather Satellites

Now satellites are helping to forecast the weather. They are in space, and they can reach any part of the world. The satellites take pictures of the atmosphere, because this is where the weather forms. They send these pictures to the weather stations. So meteorologists can see the weather of any part of the world. From the pictures, the scientists can often say how the weather will change.

Today, nearly five hundred weather stations in sixty countries receive satellite pictures. When they receive new pictures, the meteorologists compare them with earlier ones. Perhaps they may find that the clouds have changed during the last few hours. This may mean that the weather on the ground may soon change, too. In their next weather forecast, the meteorologists can say this.

So the weather satellites are a great help to the meteorologists. Before satellites were invented, the scientists could forecast the weather for about 24 or 48 hours. Now they can make good forecasts for three or five days. Soon, perhaps, they may be able to forecast the weather for a week or more ahead.

New words

satellite /ˈsætəlait/	n.	卫星
forecast /ˈfɔːkɑːst/	n.	预测
	v.	预测
atmosphere /ˈætməsfiə/	n.	大气，空气，气氛
form /fɔːm/	n.	形式，形状
	v.	形成，组成
meteorologist /miːtjəˈrɒlədʒist/	n.	气象学家
change /tʃeindʒ/	n.	变化

	v.	改变
invent /ɪnˈvent/	vt.	发明
perhaps /pəˈhæps/	adv.	也许

Phrases and expressions

compare … with …	比较
take pictures	拍照
any part of the world	世界上的任何一个角落

Reading comprehension

Choose the one that best completes each of the following statements according to the text.

(1) Satellites travel _____.

    A. in space

    B. in the atmosphere

    C. above the ground

    D. above space

(2) Why do we use the weather satellites to take pictures of the atmosphere? Because _____.

    A. the weather satellites can do it easily

    B. clouds form there

    C. the weather forms there

    D. the pictures can forecast the weather

(3) Meteorologists forecast the weather _____.

    A. when they have received satellite pictures

    B. after they have compared new satellite pictures with earlier ones

    C. before they received satellite pictures

    D. during their study of satellite pictures

(4) Maybe we'll soon be able to forecast the weather for _____.

    A. one day

    B. two days

    C. five days

    D. seven days or even longer

(5) The main (主要的) idea of this passage is that satellites are now used in _____.

    A. taking pictures of the atmosphere

    B. receiving pictures of the atmosphere

    C. doing other work in many ways

    D. weather forecasting

• Unit Eight　Science

现在进行时的用法

Now satellites are helping to forecast the weather. 一句中运用了现在进行时态。它的构成是：主语＋be＋动词的 ing 形式(现在分词)，即：

I＋am＋*v.* -ing

We(You,They)＋are＋*v.* -ing

He(She,It)＋is＋*v.* -ing

定义：现在进行时表示现在或当前一段时间正在进行的动作。

现在进行时的基本用法：

(1)表示现在(指说话人说话时)正在发生的事情。

We are waiting for you.

(2)习惯进行：表示长期的或重复性的动作，说话时动作未必正在进行。

Mr. Green is writing another novel.

(说话时未必在写，只处于写作的过程当中。)

She is learning piano under Mr. Smith.

(3)已经确定或安排好的将来活动。

I'm leaving for a trip in Nepal next week.(已经安排了)

We're flying to Paris tomorrow.(票已经拿到了)

情态动词的用法

情态动词是一种本身有一定的词义，但要与动词原形及其被动语态一起使用，给谓语动词增添情态色彩，表示说话人对有关行为或事物的态度和看法，认为其可能、应该或必要等。情态动词后面加动词原形。情态动词数量不多，但用途广泛，主要有：

can(could),may(might),must,need,ought to,
dare(dared),shall(should),will(would)

例如：

We should plant many trees on the mountains.

我们应该在山上种许多树。

Tables can be made of stone.

桌子可由石头做成。

Waste paper should not be thrown here.

废纸不应该扔在这里。

 Fun time

Tongue Twister

A big black bug bit a big black bear, made the big black bear bleed blood.

A big black bug bit a big black bear. Where's the big black bear the big black bug bit?

A bitter biting bittern bit a better brother bittern, and the bitter better bittern bit the bitter biter back. And the bitter bittern, bitten, by the better bitten bittern, said, "I'm a bitter biter bit, alack!"

单元复习

I 词汇练习

选择合适的词或词组填入空白处。

satellite　forecast　atmosphere　form
meteorologist　change　invent　perhaps

1. _____ I can help you.
2. On second thoughts he _____ his mind.
3. He _____ a new type of stethoscope.
4. The _____ of the city is very much polluted.
5. The number of known _____ in the solar system rose to 32.
6. He is a _____.
7. Who can _____ the future?
8. The design is _____ with triangles.

II 语法练习

用现在进行时完成下列句子。

1. What _____ you _____ (do)?
2. I _____ (sing) an English song.
3. What _____ he _____ (mend)?
4. He _____ (mend) a car.
5. _____ you _____ (fly) a kite? Yes, _____.
6. _____ she _____ (sit) in the boat?
7. _____ you _____ (ask) questions?
8. We _____ (play) games now.

III 阅读理解

阅读下面短文,根据短文内容,从短文后面每题所给的选项中选择最佳的一项。

Look at the car. It's Mr. Black's car. It doesn't work now. Mr. Black is under it. He is

• Unit Eight   Science

mending it. Mrs. Black is near the car. She is helping Mr. Black. The girl in the car is Kate, Mr. Black's daughter. Who is the boy in the car? He is Jim, Kate's brother. It's Saturday today. They don't work. They want to go to Zhongshan Park. They all look worried(着急).

1. Today is _____.
   A. Tuesday   B. Thursday
   C. Saturday   D. Monday
2. Mr. Black is _____ his car.
   A. washing   B. driving
   C. cleaning   D. mending
3. _____ is helping Mr. Black near the car.
   A. Miss Black   B. Mrs. Black
   C. Kate   D. Jim
4. Kate is _____ the car with her brother, Jim.
   A. in   B. beside
   C. under   D. near
5. They are going to a _____.
   A. zoo   B. farm
   C. factory   D. park

Unit Nine   Medicine

How much do you know about them?

1. Discussion.

(1) What should you do if you are ill?

(2) Do you want to be a doctor?

(3) Are you interested in learning how to keep fit and healthy?

(4) Are you worried about flu?

(5) What will happen to people if they do not have proper exercise?

2. Pair work: Read the following dialogue with your partner.

Nurse: Good morning.

Patient: Good morning.

Nurse: What seems to be the problem?

Patient: I'm running a high fever and feeling terribly bad.

Nurse: How long have you had the problem?

Patient: Since last night.

Nurse: Well, have you ever been here before?

Patient: As a matter of fact, I have just moved to this city.

Nurse: OK. In that case, you have to fill in this registration card. Your age, gender, address and things like that.

Patient: No problem. Which department should I register with, madam?

• Unit Nine   Medicine

Nurse: You'd better go to the medical department.
Patient: Here is my registration card.
Nurse: Thank you. The registration fee is one dollar.

A Hospital for Teddy

You might go to the hospital if you're ill. You may think it is a little scary to go to a hospital. But doctors and nurses in the hospital can help you feel better.

What happens inside a hospital? What do the doctors do in different departments? How do the doctors treat patients? Kids learn more about hospitals and doctors at the Teddy Bear hospital.

There is a Teddy Bear hospital in Berlin, Germany. Kids can be doctors here. Their teddy bears are their patients.

Real doctors teach the kids a lot. The doctors help the kids to examine patients and give them shots. They learn to take care of patients.

Otto is one of these kids. He lives in Berlin. He studies very hard. He is looking at an X-ray photo of his teddy bear.

New words

hospital /ˈhɔspitl/	n.	医院
scary /ˈskɛəri/	a.	引起惊慌的
department /diˈpɑːtmənt/	n.	科室
treat /triːt/	vt.	医疗,治疗(+for)
	vi.	探讨;论述(+of/about)
examine /igˈzæmin/	vt.	检查;细查;诊察
shot /ʃɔt/	n.	打针,注射
patient /ˈpeiʃənt/	n.	病人
X-ray /ˈeksrei/	n.	X光照片

Phrases and expressions

take care of   照顾

Proper names

Berlin, Germany   德国柏林

teddy bear　　　　　　泰迪熊
Otto　　　　　　　　　奥特

Reading comprehension

Decide whether the following statements are true(T)or false(F)according to the text.
(　　)(1)We might go to the hospital if we're ill.
(　　)(2)Doctors and nurses in the hospital can help patients feel better.
(　　)(3)There is no Teddy Bear hospital in China now.
(　　)(4)There is a Teddy Bear hospital in Berlin.
(　　)(5)Otto is a child.

Grammar

英语中的存在句型

"There is a Teddy Bear hospital in Berlin, Germany."
there be 表示"存在有",即当我们告诉某人某事存在(或不存在)常用这种结构。其中 there 是引导词,本身无词义;be 为谓语动词,后面跟的是名词,也就是主语,也就是说 there be 结构的运用也就是倒装的具体运用。其真正的主语在 there be 之后。

一、注意事项
(1)there be 结构中的 be 是可以运用各种时态的。
There is going to be a meeting tonight.
今晚有个会议。
There was a knock at the door.
有人敲门。
There will be rain soon.
不久天就要下雨了。
(2)动词 be 单复数形式要跟 there be 之后的真正的主语一致,并且要根据就近一致原则来变换 be 的单复数形式。
There is a book on the desk.
课桌上有一本书。
How many people are there in the city?
这个城市里有多少人口?
There is a pen and two books on the desk.
课桌上有一支钢笔和两本书。
There are two books and a pen on the desk.
课桌上有两本书和一支钢笔。
(3)在 there be 引起的句子结构中,用来修饰主语的不定式用主动形式和被动形式均可。
There is no time to lose(＝to be lost). 时间紧迫。

There is nothing to see(＝to be seen).看不见有什么。

There is nothing to do.(＝to be done).无事可做。

二、结构变形

在 there be 结构中还可把 be 改变,从而使得 there be 结构有了一些改变。具体总结如下。

(1)There used/seem/happen/appear to be。

There might be snow at night.

晚上可能有雪。

There appeared to be nobody willing to help.

看来没人愿意帮忙。

There used to be a building here.

过去这儿有一座楼房。

There happened to be a man walking by.

碰巧有个人在此经过。

There doesn't seem to be much hope.

好像没有太大的希望。

(2)在 there be 的 be 前还可以加上各种情态动词。

There must be something wrong.

一定有问题。

There ought not to be so many people.

不应该有这么多的人。

There might still be hope.

可能还有点希望。

(3)在 there be 句型中的 be 还可以换成其他的动词与 there 连用,这些词都是表示状态的,如:live,stand,exist,remain 等;或用来描写某事的发生或某人的到达,如:come,appear,enter,follow,occur 等。

There lived a rich man.

这以前住着一个富翁。

Then there came a knock at the door.

然后有人敲门。

Long,long ago,there lived a king.

很久很久以前,这里有一个国王。

There followed a terrible noise.

然后是传来了可怕的声音。

Suddenly there entered a strange man.

突然进来了一个奇怪的人。

三、特殊的表达方式

(1)There is no sense in doing 做某事是没有用的、没有意义的。

There is no sense in making him angry.

让他生气是没有用的。

There is no sense in going alone.

一个人去是没有好处的。

(2) There is no use/good doing 做某事是没有用的、没有必要的。

There is no use trying to explain it.

解释是没有必要的。

There is no good/use going there.

去那儿是没有好处的。

(3) There is no need to do sth. 没有必要做某事。

There is no need to worry.

没有必要担心。

There is no need to give him so much money.

根本没有必要给他那么多的钱。

(4) There is thought/said/reported to be 人们认为有/据说有/据报道有。

There is thought to be a war between these two countries.

人们认为在这两国之间有一场战争。

There is reported to be a better way to cure cancer.

据报道，找到了一种更好的治疗癌症的方法。

(5) There is no doing (口语) 不可能……

There is no telling when he will be back.

无法知道他什么时候回来。

There is no knowing what he is doing.

无法知道他在做什么。

Tom's Excuse

Teacher: Tom, why are you late for school every day?

Tom: Every time I come to the corner, a sign says, "School—Go Slow."

单元复习

I 词汇练习

选择合适的词或词组填入空白处。

  hospital scary department treat examine shot patient X-ray

1. He gave me a chest _____ and took my blood pressure.

2. His sick father is in _____.
3. She put worms, snakes and other _____ things into a pot.
4. Do not _____ this serious matter as a joke.
5. The doctor is very _____ with his patients.
6. The doctor _____ the boy and found there was nothing the matter with him.
7. The policeman fired a warning _____.
8. She's the head of the firm's personnel _____.

Ⅱ 语法练习

用 is, are 填空。

1. There _____ a nurse in the ward.
2. There _____ some milk in the bottle.
3. There _____ some boys under the tree.
4. There _____ a driver in that bus.
5. There _____ not any teachers in the office now.
6. There _____ many trees in the park.
7. There _____ not any sheep near the house.
8. There _____ five pupils in the classroom.
9. There _____ not a cinema near our school.
10. There _____ two plates in the cupboard.

Ⅲ 阅读理解

阅读下面短文,根据短文内容,从短文后面每题所给的选项中选择最佳的一项。

John is a paper boy. He delivers(投递)newspapers to different houses in his street every day. He has about 80 customers(客户). Half of his customers only take the newspapers on weekdays, and about half take the newspapers on weekdays and on Sundays. Two of John's customers only take the newspapers on Sundays.

John has to get up at 4:30 every morning to deliver his newspapers. It takes longer to deliver the newspapers on Sundays. The Sunday newspapers are twice as heavy as those on weekdays. John is saving his money to buy a new bicycle. He is also saving money for college (大学). He has already saved 500 dollars.

1. John _____ every day.
   A. reads books   B. sells newspapers
   C. borrows books   D. delivers newspapers
2. How many customers does he have?
   A. About 40.   B. About 120.
   C. About 80.   D. About 20.

3. _____ of his customers only take the newspapers on Sundays.
   A. Two   B. Eighty
   C. Forty   D. Twenty
4. What time does he have to get up every morning?
   A. 3:30.   B. 4:30.
   C. 5:30.   D. 6:30.
5. John is saving money by buying _____.
   A. a newspaper   B. a new bag
   C. a house   D. a new bicycle

Unit Ten Childhood

Do you remember those days?

1. Discussion.

(1) How about your childhood?

(2) Who was your best friend when you were a child?

(3) Did you like playing games when you were a child?

(4) Are there any interesting stories you know about a child?

(5) How old were you when you entered pre-school?

2. Pair work: Read the following dialogue with your partner.

Tom: Hi, Jack.

Jack: Oh, Tom, Nice to meet you!

Tom: Nice to meet you, too. This is my sister, Lily.

Jack: Oh, hello! I'm afraid we have seen each other before, do you remember me?

Lily: Er, I'm afraid I forget it. I'm sorry, but when did that happen?

Jack: A summer about six years ago. We both studied in a piano training. I remember you played the piano very well.

Lily: Oh, let me think about it. You are that humorous brother. Glad to see you again.

Tom: So you two knew each other before. It's so good.

Jack: I really don't know that you two are sister and brother.

Lily: So let's celebrate that we meet again.
Jack: Good idea.
Tom: OK, let's go.

扫一扫跟着练

Susan

Last week, my four-year-old daughter, Susan, was invited to a children's party. I decided to take her by train.

Susan was very excited because she had never travelled on a train before. She sat near the window and asked questions about everything she saw.

Suddenly, a middle-aged lady got on the train and sat opposite Susan. "Hello, little girl," she said. Susan did not answer, but looked at her curiously. The lady was dressed in a blue coat and a large, funny hat. After the train had left the station, the lady opened her handbag and took out her powder compact. She then began to make up her face. "Why are you doing that?" Susan asked. "To make myself beautiful," the lady answered. She put away her compact and smiled kindly.

"But you are still ugly," Susan said. Susan was amused, but I was very embarrassed!

扫一扫跟着练

middle-aged /ˈmɪdlˌeɪdʒd/	adj.	中年的
opposite /ˈɒpəzɪt/	prep.	在……对面
curiously /ˈkjʊəriəsli/	adv.	好奇地
funny /ˈfʌni/	adj.	可笑的，滑稽的
powder /ˈpaʊdə/	n.	香粉
compact /ˈkɒmpækt/	n.	带镜的化妆盒
kindly /ˈkaɪndli/	adv.	和蔼地
ugly /ˈʌgli/	adj.	丑陋的
amused /əˈmjuːzd/	adj.	有趣的
smile /smaɪl/	v.	微笑
embarrassed /ɪmˈbærəst/	adj.	尴尬的，窘迫的

Phrases and expressions

get on	登上
look at	看，盯着看
take out	拿出来，取出来

be dressed in…	穿戴着……
make up	为……化妆

Reading comprehension

Answer the following questions according to the text.

(1) How old is Susan?
_____

(2) Why was Susan very excited?
_____

(3) Where was the lady?
_____

(4) Was the lady beautiful or not?
_____

(5) What did the lady do?
_____

Grammar

一般过去时态

一般过去时态：表示过去某一时间所发生的动作或存在的状态。谓语动词要用一般过去式。经常与 yesterday（昨天），last week（上周），last month（上个月），last year（去年），two months ago（两个月前），the day before yesterday（前天），in 1990（在 1990 年），in those days（在那些日子里）等表示过去的时间状语连用。

I was born in 1990.
我出生在 1990 年。
When did you go to the park?
你是什么时候去公园的?
I went to the park last week.
我是上周去的公园。

在上面的句子中，第一句属于系动词 be 的一般过去时态；第二句和第三句属于实义动词的一般过去时态。

系动词 be 的一般过去时态：在没有实义动词的句子中使用系动词 be。am/is 的过去式为 was；are 的过去式为 were。

构成：
(1) 肯定句：主语＋was (were)＋表语。
I was late yesterday.
昨天我迟到了。

(2)否定句:主语＋was（were）＋not＋表语。

We weren't late yesterday.

我们昨天没迟到。

(3)疑问句:was（were）＋主语＋表语。

Were you ill yesterday?

你昨天病了吗?

① 肯定回答:Yes,I was.(是的,我病了。)

② 否定句:No,I wasn't.(不,我没病。)

(4)特殊疑问句:特殊疑问词＋was（were）＋主语＋表语。

When were you born?

你是什么时候出生的?

Fun time

First Flight

Mr. Johnson had never been up in an airplane before and he had read a lot about air accidents, so one day when a friend offered to take him for a ride in his own small plane, Mr. Johnson was very worried about accepting. Finally, however, his friend persuaded him that it was very safe, and Mr. Johnson boarded the plane.

His friend started the engine and began to taxi onto the runway of the airport. Mr. Johnson had heard that the most dangerous part of a flight was the take－off and the landing, so he was extremely frightened and closed his eyes.

After a minute or two he opened them again, looked out of the window of the plane, and said to his friend, "Look at those people down there. They look as small as ants, don't they?"

"Those are ants," answered his friend. "We're still on the ground."

单元复习

I 词汇练习

选择合适的词或词组填入空白处。

excited middle-aged opposite curiously funny

powder kindly ugly smile embarrassed

1. She is very _____ about winning the first prize.

2. The _____ boy fiddled with his hat.

3. He is a _____ man.

4. He has a _____ manner.
5. He looked _____ at the people.
6. That's the _____ joke I've ever heard.
7. There's too much _____ on your nose.
8. What are you _____ at?
9. What an _____ building!
10. They have _____ views on the question.

Ⅱ 语法练习

请用动词的正确形式填空。

1. I _____ (have) an exciting party last weekend.
2. _____ she _____ (practice) her guitar yesterday? No, she _____.
3. What _____ Tom _____ (do) on Saturday evening?
   He _____ (watch) TV and _____ (read) an interesting book.
4. They all _____ (go) to the mountains yesterday morning.
5. She _____ (not visit) her aunt last weekend.
   She _____ (stay) at home and _____ (do) some cleaning.
6. When _____ you _____ (write) this song? I _____ (write) it last year.
7. My friend, Carol, _____ (study) for the math test and _____ (practice) English last night.
8. _____ Mr. Li _____ (do) the project on Monday morning? Yes, he _____.
9. How _____ (be) Jim's weekend? It _____ (be not) bad.
10. _____ (be) your mother a sales assistant last year? No, she _____.

Ⅲ 阅读理解

阅读下面短文，根据短文内容，从短文后面每题所给的选项中选择最佳的一项。

  The students were having their chemistry(化学) class. Miss Li was telling the children what water was like. After that, she asked her students, "What's water?" No one spoke for a few minutes. Miss Li asked again, "Why don't you answer my question? Didn't I tell you what water is like?"

  Just then a boy put up his hand and said, "Miss Li, you told us that water has no colour and no smell. But where to find such kind of water? The water in the river behind my house is always black and it has a bad smell." Most of the children agreed with him.

  "I'm sorry, children," said the teacher, "Our water is getting dirtier and dirtier. That's a problem."

1. The students were having their _____ class.
  A. English   B. Chinese   C. chemistry   D. maths

77

2. Miss Li was telling the children what _____ was like.
   A. water
   B. air
   C. earth
   D. weather
3. A boy said, "The water in the river behind my house is always _____."
   A. white
   B. black
   C. clean
   D. clear
4. Most of the children _____ the boy.
   A. agreed with
   B. wrote to
   C. heard from
   D. sent for
5. The water in the river has colour and smell because it is getting _____.
   A. more and more
   B. less and less
   C. cleaner and cleaner
   D. dirtier and dirtier

Unit Eleven Computer

Warming up

Do you often use computers?

1. Discussion.

(1) Do you know how to use computers?
(2) Do you know what a computer can do?
(3) Do you know how many types of computers there are?
(4) Do you know what are digital and analog computers?
(5) Have you heard of IBM, Microsoft and Windows?

2. Pair work: Read the following dialogue with your partner.

Jennifer: Sam, why do we seldom see you now?
　　Sam: Oh, I've been busy with my new computer.
Jennifer: Is that so? Then you must have learned a lot about how to use one.
　　Sam: Not much, I'm afraid. To tell you the truth, I mostly play games on it.
Jennifer: I've been using my computer a lot. I use it for all kinds of things.
　　Sam: Really? What else can I do with it at home?
Jennifer: A great many things. For example, you can use it to send or receive e-mail. You can also use it to find the information you need.
　　Sam: Really? How can I do these things?
Jennifer: Just connect your computer to the Internet.

Sam: I've heard a lot about the Internet. But I don't understand it and I don't know how to make use of it, either.

Jennifer: The Internet is a wonderful information network. When your computer is on line, you can communicate with anyone who is on it. You can have access to all the data in the world.

Sam: I see. I'll try to do these things with my computer as soon as possible.

 Text

The Age of Computer

One of the greatest advances in modern technology is the invention of computers. Today they are widely used in industry, research institutes, offices and homes. Computers are capable of doing extremely complicated work in all branches of science. They can solve the most complex mathematical problems, or put thousands of unrelated facts in order. They can be put to different uses. They work accurately and at high speed, they save research workers years of hard work.

An expert on automation once said that it was a mistake to believe that machines operated by computers could think. There is no possibility that human beings will be controlled by machines. No computers are capable of learning from their mistakes and improving on their performance. They need detailed instructions from human beings in order to be able to operate. They can never lead independent lives or rule the world by making decisions of their own.

Ordinary people can use computers to obtain valuable information. For instance, people could be informed about weather conditions. Computers can also be used in hospitals. By providing a machine with the patient's symptoms, the doctor would be able to diagnose the nature of his illness. Bookkeepers and accountants also could be relieved of dull work, for the boring task of compiling and checking lists of figures could be done entirely by machines.

Computers are the best servants man has ever had, and there is no limit to the ways in which they can be used to improve our lives.

New words

advance /əd'vɑːns/	n.	前进，进展
invention /in'venʃən/	n.	发明
widely /'waidli/	adv.	广泛地，普遍地
research /ri'sɜːtʃ/	n.	研究，调查
institute /'institjuːt/	n.	学会，协会，学院

Unit Eleven　Computer

complicated /ˈkɔmplikeitid/	adj.	复杂的,难解的
branch /brɑːntʃ/	n.	分支,分科
complex /ˈkɔmpleks/	adj.	复杂的
mathematical /ˌmæθəˈmætikl/	adj.	数学的
unrelated /ˌʌnriˈleitid/	adj.	无关的,没有关系的
accurately /ˈækjuritli/	adv.	准确地,精确地
automation /ˌɔːtəˈmeiʃən/	n.	自动化
operate /ˈɔpəreit/	v.	操作,运转,开动,起作用
detailed /diˈteild/	adj.	详细的,详尽的
instruction /inˈstrkʃən/	n.	指示,用法说明(书),指令
independent /ˌindiˈpendənt/	adj.	独立自主的
ordinary /ˈɔːdnri/	adj.	普通的,平凡的
obtain /əbˈtein/	vt.	获得,得到
valuable /ˈvæljuəbl/	adj.	贵重的,有价值的
information /ˌinfəˈmeiʃən/	n.	信息,情报,知识
condition /kənˈdiʃən/	n.	情况;状态
inform /inˈfɔːm/	n.	告知,通知;为……提供信息、情报
symptom /ˈsimptəm/	n.	征兆,症候
diagnose /ˈdaiəgnəuz/	vt.	诊断
accountant /əˈkauntənt/	n.	会计人员,会计师
relieve /riˈliːv/	vt.	减轻,解除
dull /dʌl/	adj.	无趣的,呆滞的,单调的
boring /ˈbɔːriŋ/	adj.	令人厌烦的,乏味的
compile /kəmˈpail/	vt.	编辑,汇编,【电脑】编译(程序);转化成机器语言
list /list/	n.	目录,名单,数据清单
figure /ˈfigə/	n.	图形,图表,插图;数字

Phrases and expressions

be capable of	能够(做)
put ... in order	将……排列整齐
at high speed	高速地,快速地
learn from	向……学习
in order to	为了
make decisions of one's own	自己作决定
for instance	例如,以……为例
inform about	通知,告诉,告知

Reading comprehension

Choose the one that best completes each of the following statements according to the text.

(1) According to the first paragraph, why can computers save research workers years of hard work?

A. Because computers can work accurately and at high speed.

B. Because computers can solve the most complex mathematical problems.

C. Because computers can put thousands of unrelated facts in order.

(2) Which of the following is correct?

A. Human beings will be controlled by computers in the future.

B. Machines operated by computers could not think like human beings.

C. Computers can also learn from mistakes they have made.

(3) In order to operate, computers _____.

A. need detailed instructions from human beings

B. can make decisions by themselves

C. may send instructions to human beings

(4) The third paragraph mainly tells us that _____.

A. ordinary people can use computers to obtain valuable information

B. computers can be used in hospitals

C. computers can be used widely

(5) The last paragraph means that _____.

A. computers are the best servants at home

B. computers can be used to improve our lives in various ways

C. computers can not help to improve our lives

 Grammar

动词不定式汇总

动词不定式是由"to＋动词原形"构成的一种非谓语动词结构。不定式是一种非限定性动词，而非限定动词是指那些在句中不能单独充当谓语的动词。有些动词不定式不带 to，动词不定式可以作句子的主语、表语、宾语、定语、补语、状语或单独使用。不定式保留动词的某些特性，可以有自己的宾语、状语等。动词不定式和它后面的宾语、状语等一起构成短语，叫做不定式短语。

一、用作主语

直接把动词不定式置于句首的情况不多，多数情况用 it 作形式主语，把真正的主语——动词不定式置于句末，特别是不定式短语较长时。动词不定式作主语，谓语动词用第三人称单数形式。

To see is to believe.

百闻不如一见。

To get there by bike will take us half an hour.

骑车到那儿需要半小时。

It's so nice to hear your voice.

听到你的声音真高兴。

二、用作表语

动词不定式作表语,常说明主语的内容、性质、特征。

My chief purpose is to point out the difficulties of the matter.

我的主要意图是指出这件事情的困难所在。

三、用作宾语

(1)可以接带 to 的动词不定式作宾语的动词主要有:要求、选择、同意(ask,choose,agree),期望、决定、学习(expect,hope,decide,learn),宁可、假装、知道(prefer,pretend,know),希望、想要、愿意(wish,want,would like/love)。

I hope to be back soon.

我希望早点回家?

I happen to know the answer to your question.

我碰巧知道你那道问题的答案

(2)跟"疑问句+带 to 的不定式"结构作宾语的动词常见的有 decide,know,learn,show,teach,tell 等。

Please show us how to do that.

请演示给我们如何去做。

Do you know how to play bridge?

你知道怎么打桥牌吗?

(3)动词 feel,find,make,think 等后面,可以用 it 作形式宾语代替真正的宾语——动词不定式,句子结构是 … feel/find/make/… it+$adj./n.$+to do… 。

I find it difficult to remember everything.

我发现将这一切全记住很难。

四、用作定语

句子的主语或宾语是动词不定式的逻辑主语,不定式与其所修饰的名词、代词等存在逻辑的动宾关系时,此时动词不定式作定语。

I have so many chores to do today.

我今天有很多家务事要做。

I can't think of any good advice to give her.

不能给她想出任何好办法。

There are still many things to do there.

那里仍有许多事情要做。

五、用作补语

动词不定式作补语时,在主动语态句里补宾语,在被动语态句里补主语,句子的宾语或主语是不定式动作的逻辑执行者。如果不定式是 to be done,句子的宾语或主语就是逻辑承受者。

在主、被动语态句里用带 to 的动词不定式作补语的动词主要有:要求、允许、提议(ask,

allow,permit,advise),期望、邀请、鼓励(expect,suppose,invite,encourage),教导、告诉、想要(teach,tell,want),等待、希望、愿意(wait for,wish,would like/love)等。

I expected him to arrive on Saturday.

我估计他星期六到达。

She encouraged me to try again.

她鼓励我再试一次。

六、用作状语

不定式可用作状语,表示目的、原因、结果等。

A friend of my came to see me last night.(目的)

昨晚有个朋友来看我。

Be careful not to catch cold.(目的)

小心别着凉了。

We jumped with joy to hear it.(原因)

听到这个消息我们都高兴得跳了起来。

To hear him talk in that manner,you would think he's a foreigner.(原因)

听他这样讲话,你会以为他是外国人。

He left,never to return.(结果)

他走了,再也没回来。

 Fun time

He Must Have a Computer

A mother was teaching her 5-year-old son about God.

"Do you know," she said to him one day, "that God knows where everybody is all the time, and exactly what they are doing."

The little boy looked at his mother wide-eyed and said, "Wow! He must have a computer."

单元复习

I 词汇练习

单项选择,选出一个能填入空白处的最佳选项。

1. He had about 6,000 _____ including the electric light bulb, the phonograph, and the mimeograph machine.

    A. inventions   B. makings   C. mechanics

Unit Eleven Computer

2. His father works in the largest _____ institute in this city.
   A. researching   B. research   C. complex
3. Are you _____ of climbing that tree?
   A. capable   B. going   C. enjoying
4. It is rather _____, I couldn't solve it without help.
   A. problem   B. complicated   C. big
5. The key _____ was how to move the heavy machinery immediately.
   A. case   B. situation   C. problem
6. We should _____ oil, or else there won't be any left in the world.
   A. save   B. use   C. develop
7. He is driving _____ a speed of eighty miles an hour.
   A. in   B. at   C. for
8. _____ yourself; don't get angry.
   A. Control   B. Ease   C. Find
9. The boss gave me so many _____ at one time that I got muddled up.
   A. instructions   B. instruction   C. information
10. I am sorry, I haven't made my own _____.
    A. decision   B. word   C. view

II 语法练习

用不定式结构就以下所给的词汇造句。

1. promise, be present at the ceremony

   _____

2. remember, send my regards to her

   _____

3. discuss, where to go for an outing

   _____

4. teach, how, make use of reference books

   _____

5. not, advisable, read such difficult things at this stage

   _____

6. quite possible, catch up with the other groups

   _____

7. shame, not, be able to give them any help

   _____

8. an honour, have this chance to speak here

   _____

9. form a special board, examine the problem

   _____

10. what, do, improve your handwriting

Ⅲ 阅读理解

阅读下面短文，根据短文内容，从短文后面每题所给的选项中选择最佳的一项。

Almost everyone in the world uses oil(石油) in some way. Without oil, the world will stop, so men look for it everywhere. Oilmen drill for oil in deserts(沙漠), in mountains and under the sea. Quite often they find nothing, but the search(寻找) for oil always goes on. Oil is very important because none of our machines can run without it. Big ships carry oil everywhere. Perhaps the oil in your bicycle or in your father's car has come from somewhere far away. Perhaps it has come from Iraq(伊拉克) or Venezuela(委内瑞拉). Cars and bicycles need oil, but so do many other things. How many things can you name?

1. _____ oil in some way in the world.
   A. Most people use   B. Hardly anyone uses
   C. All people use   D. Few people use

2. In the passage, "drill" means _____.
   A. 操练   B. 练习
   C. 钻探   D. 开采

3. Oilmen sometimes find oil _____.
   A. in deserts   B. in mountains
   C. under the sea   D. A, B and C

4. Oilmen _____ oil all the time.
   A. look up   B. look for
   C. look into   D. look out

5. The sentence "Big ships carry oil everywhere." tells us _____.
   A. oil comes from everywhere   B. oil comes from big ships
   C. oil is needed everywhere   D. big ships need oil everywhere

Unit Twelve Work

 Warming up

I. Discussion

1. What does your father or mother do?
2. What does your father or mother work for?
3. What do you think most people work for?
4. What are you going to do in the future?
5. What are you going to work for?

II. Pair work: Read the following dialogue with your partner.

Jane: We've got a new manager in our department.
Larry: Oh? You hoped to get that job, didn't you?
Jane: Yes, I did.
Larry: I'm sorry. That's too bad. Who is it? Who got the job, I mean?

Jane: Someone called Drexier, Carl Drexier, a tall, handsome man. But he's been with the company only two years. I've been here longer. And I know more about the job, too.

Larry: Hmm. Why do you think they passed you over?

Jane: Because I'm a woman, of course! It isn't fair.

Larry: Well, maybe there's something else … What kind of clothes does he wear?

Jane: He's always dressed in a dark suit, a white shirt and a tie. Why?

Larry: Perhaps that has something to do with it.

Jane: You think I didn't get the job because I come to work in jeans and a sweater?

Larry: It's possible, isn't it? You just look too casual to be in an important position.

 Text

Work While You Work, Play While You Play

The proverb "Work while you work, play while you play" is useful to people in all walks of life. A proper and normal daily life signifies order, progress and cheerfulness.

School life is more or less regular. Students have class hours at certain times of a day, and go to the playground after school. Most of the school children are healthy, cheerful and progressive, because they are trained according to their properly regulated daily program.

Nowadays, many businessmen and officials also have office hours. During that time, they work very hard and think about nothing except work. But when they are free, they will go to places where they can relax themselves and have fun. If they are not successful people, they may not be able to afford the time and money.

In short, the proverb "Work while you work, play while you play" should be strictly observed by anyone who wishes to make his life pleasant, efficient and successful. When our mind is concentrated on one thing, it will surely work efficiently. In this way, you will have time to settle other problems. It is true that one cannot work all day long. Play is as important as work. When you play, you will feel fresh and cheerful so that you may not be sick of your work. So if you can, give yourself enough time to play. And always remember the proverb "Work while you work, play while you play."

Unit Twelve　Work

New words

扫一扫跟着练

while /hwail/	conj.	当……的时候,与此同时
proverb /ˈprɔvəːb/	n.	谚语,格言
proper /ˈprɔpə/	adj.	适当的,正确的
normal /ˈnɔːməl/	adj.	正常的,通常的
daily /ˈdeili/	adj.	每日的,日常的
signify /ˈsignifai/	v.	表示,象征,意味,预示
progress /ˈprəugres/	n.	进步,发展,进展
cheerfulness /ˈtʃiəfulnis/	n.	高兴,愉快
regular /ˈregjulə/	adj.	规律的,正规的
certain /ˈsəːtn/	adj.	某一,确定的
playground /ˈpleigraund/	n.	运动场,游乐场
cheerful /ˈtʃiəful/	adj.	高兴的,愉快的
progressive /prəˈgresiv/	adj.	进步的,增长的
properly /ˈprɔpəli/	adv.	正确地,适当地
regulate /ˈregjuːleit/	v.	使有条理,调整,规定
nowadays /ˈnauədeiz/	adv.	现在,当前
businessman /ˈbiznismæn/	n.	生意人,商人
official /əˈfiʃəl/	n.	公务员,职员,官员
	adj.	官方的,正式的,有权威的
relax /riˈlæks/	v.	放松,舒畅
afford /əˈfɔːd/	v.	承担得起,支付得起
strictly /ˈstriktli/	adv.	严谨地,严厉地,精确地
observe /əbˈzəːv/	v.	遵守,观察,注意
efficient /iˈfiʃənt/	adj.	效率高的,能胜任的,有能力的
mind /maind/	n.	意识,注意力,思想
concentrate /ˈkɔnsentreit/	v.	集中,专心
efficiently /iˈfiʃəntli/	adv.	高效率地,有效地
fresh /freʃ/	adj.	新鲜的,精力充沛的
sick /sik/	adj.	病的,恶心的,厌倦的
enough /iˈnʌf/	adj.	足够的,充分的

Phrases and expressions

walk of life	行业,职业
more or less	或多或少,左右
at the time of	在……的时候
according to	根据

in short 简而言之,总之
concentrate on 集中于……上,聚精会神于……
all day long 整天
so that 于是,结果是

Reading comprehension

Choose the one that best completes each of the following statements according to the text.

1. Which of the following is not a program in a normal daily life?
   A. Going to work by train.
   B. Going to see the doctor after school.
   C. Washing up at night.

2. Whose everyday life is not properly regulated?
   A. Office workers'.
   B. A sales manager's.
   C. Some school children's.

3. If we work all day long, we will _____.
   A. make progress
   B. be efficient
   C. get sick

4. Our mind will surely work efficiently if it is concentrated on _____.
   A. one thing only
   B. as many things as it can
   C. work and play at the same time

5. To become a successful person, one must know how to _____.
   A. earn more money   B. get help from others   C. live a healthy life

Grammar

一般将来时

1. 概述

一般将来时表示将来某个时间要发生的动作或存在的状态。

2. 构成

一般将来时由"助动词 will/shall＋动词原形"构成。will 用于第二、三人称,shall 用于第一人称。在口语中,will 在名词或代词后常缩写为"'ll",而 will not 则简缩为 won't。但在美国英语中,各种人称皆可用 will。例如:

He will help his sister with her lessons.
他将帮助他妹妹做功课。

We won't be free this afternoon.

今天下午我们没空。

3. 一般将来时的用法

(1)表示未来的动作或存在的状态,常与表示将来的时间状语连用,如 tomorrow, next Sunday, soon, in a month, in the future 等。例如:

We shall leave for London next Monday.

我们将在下周一去伦敦。

He will come to see you the day after tomorrow.

后天他要来看你。

You will be 20 next year.

明年你就 20 岁了。

(2)表示将来反复发生的动作或习惯性动作。例如:

We shall come and work in this factory every year.

我们将每年来这工厂参加劳动。

The students will have five English classes per week this term.

本学期学生每周将要上 5 节英语课。

4. 一般将来时的其他表达法

(1)"be going to+动词原形"表将来:

① 这种结构表示打算、计划、决定要做的事或肯定要发生的事。例如:

What are you going to do next Sunday?

下星期天你打算干什么?

They are going to meet outside the school gate.

他们打算在校门口外见面。

② 还可表示说话人根据已有的事实或迹象,认为某事即将发生、肯定会发生或可能出现的情况。例如:

I think I'm going to die.

我想我要死了。(现在生命垂危。)

Look at the cloud. It's going to rain.

瞧那乌云,天要下雨了。(看到乌云密布,从而断定天要下雨。)

The ice is going to break.

冰就要破了。

③这种结构表示肯定、预测、注定会等情况时可以和 think, hope, want, believe, like 等表示静态的动词连用。例如:

He failed in the exam; he knew he was going to when he looked at the test paper.

他没考及格。他一看试卷就知道考不及格。

The question is going to be very complex.

这个问题将会很复杂。

The voters aren't going to like him.

选民们不会喜欢他的。

(2)用现在进行时来表示将来:

现在进行时表示按计划、安排即将发生的动作,这一结构常用于表示位置转移的动词,如

come，go，leave，start，move，arrive 等，还有 join，play，eat，work，return，take，wear，stay，sleep，meet 等。常与表示将来的时间状语连用。例如：

I'm leaving for Tibet on Sunday.

星期天我要去西藏。

When are you going back to your factory?

你什么时候回工厂？

He is not coming.

他不来了。

They are arriving tomorrow afternoon.

他们明天下午到达。

(3)"be about to＋动词原形"表将来：

"be about to＋动词原形"表示打算或据安排即将发生的动作。它不与表示时间的副词或其他时间状语连用。例如：

The English evening is about to start.

英语晚会即将开始。

They are about to set out.（不能说"They are about to set out soon."）

他们就要出发。

The ship is about to sail.

轮船马上就要起航。

(4)"be to＋动词原形"表将来：

"be to＋动词原形"表示约定的、计划中的或按职责、义务要求要发生的动作。这种动作通常是人的意志所能控制的，或用于征求意见。例如：

There's to be a slide show this afternoon.

今天下午要放幻灯片。

You are to hand in your papers by 10 o'clock.

到 10 点你得交上试卷。

If a man is to succeed，he must work as hard as he can.

一个人要想成功，他就必须拼命干。

1. He who seizes the right moment is the right man.
   谁把握机遇，谁就心想事成。

2. Man struggles upwards；water flows downwards.
   人往高处走，水往低处流。

3. Man errs as long as he strives.
   失误是进取的代价。

4. Actions speak louder than words.
   事实胜于雄辩。

Unit Twelve Work

5. Adversity leads to prosperity.
   穷则思变。

单元复习

I 词汇练习

Make the best choice for each of the following sentences.

1. The Internet is benefiting people in all _____.
   A. careers   B. walks of life   C. jobs
2. It is rush hour. You can't find seats on the subway train at this time _____.
   A. in a day   B. of today   C. of the day
3. They are the _____ customers of this restaurant. They come here every weekend.
   A. usual   B. regular   C. good
4. A doctor's job is _____ painstaking.
   A. more   B. less   C. more or less
5. _____ the girls in big cities like to watch fashion show programs on TV.
   A. Most   B. Most of   C. More of
6. The man-made satellite can send radio waves, _____ the engineer.
   A. according to   B. said   C. as to
7. "The Evening News" is a _____ newspaper.
   A. every day   B. everyday's   C. daily
8. To respect the elderly is a tradition _____ by the Chinese.
   A. observed   B. kept   C. taken
9. Turn off the radio, please. I can't concentrate _____ my study when it is on.
   A. on   B. to   C. at
10. The computer is not very expensive today. Many people can _____ it.
    A. pay   B. spend   C. afford

II 语法练习

Read each of the sentences and then make the best choice.

1. There _____ a meeting tomorrow afternoon.
   A. will be going to
   B. will going to be
   C. is going to be
   D. will go to be

93

2. Charlie _____ here next month.
   A. isn't working   B. doesn't working
   C. isn't going to working   D. won't work
3. Mother _____ me a nice present on my next birthday.
   A. will gives   B. will give
   C. gives   D. give
4. _____ a concert next Saturday?
   A. There will be   B. Will there be
   C. There can be   D. There are
5. If they come, we _____ a meeting.
   A. have   B. will have
   C. had   D. would have
6. If it _____ tomorrow, we'll go roller-skating.
   A. isn't rain   B. won't rain
   C. doesn't rain   D. doesn't fine
7. We _____ the work this way next time.
   A. do   B. will do
   C. going to do   D. will doing
8. My family _____ to church next weekend.
   A. will go   B. goes
   C. will going   D. is going to
9. They _____ an English evening next Sunday.
   A. are having   B. are going to have
   C. will having   D. is going to have
10. _____ you _____ free next Sunday?
    A. Will; are   B. Will; be
    C. Do; be   D. Are; be
11. —Shall I come again tomorrow afternoon?
    —_____（好的）.
    A. Yes, please   B. Yes, you will.
    C. No, please.   D. No, you won't.
12. It _____ the year of the horse next year.
    A. is going to be   B. is going to
    C. will be   D. will is
13. _____ open the window?
    A. Will you please   B. Please will you
    C. You please   D. Do you
14. It _____ us a long time to learn English well.
    A. takes   B. will take
    C. spends   D. will spend

15. The train _____ at 11.

   A. going to arrive B. will be arrive

   C. is going to D. is arriving

Ⅲ 阅读理解

Read the passage and then choose the best choice for each of the questions.

It took David several months to save up seven dollars. He wanted to buy a model plane and went to the shop with the money.

On the way, David saw a little boy crying on a corner of the street. "Why are you crying?" David asked.

"Three big boys took away my four dollars just then," the boy said. "I was on my way to buy some exercise books, but now I can't."

David thought of his seven dollars in his pocket. He thought of the model plane as well as the poor boy.

David wanted to go away, but he did not. At last he gave four dollars to the boy and went home.

1. How did David get the seven dollars?

   A. His father gave it to him. B. He worked for it.

   C. He saved it. D. He picked it up on the way home.

2. On the way to the shop, David met _____.

   A. a young girl B. his teacher

   C. a little boy D one of his friends

3. What did David want to buy?

   A. Some exercise books. B. A model plane.

   C. Clothes. D. A pair of shoes.

4. David didn't buy the model plane because _____.

   A. the shop was too far away from his home

   B. it was too expensive for him

   C. it was not so good

   D. he gave four dollars to a poor boy

5. David had only _____ dollars at last.

   A. seven B. four

   C. seventeen D. three

Unit Thirteen Film

Warming up

Do you see these films?

I. Discussion

1. Do you like seeing films?
2. What do you think of film stars?
3. Did you see the film Kungfu Panda?
4. Do you believe a poor boy can become a film star?
5. Do you like the films produced by Zhang Yimou?

II. Pair work: Read the following dialogue with your partner.

Judy: What do you two fancy seeing? There's Must Love Dogs — a romantic comedy. Oh, I love romantic comedies, don't you?

Pearl: Pride and Prejudice is on—I adore period dramas. You know all those fine ladies and gents from ages ago, long dresses and grand houses. What kind of films do you like, Ben—action, adventure, musicals?

Ben: I like films about people living in the future, on other planets.

Judy: Oh, Science Fiction—not really my thing.

Ben: Well, what about Nightmare on Elm Street?

Pearl: No, thanks. Horror films don't do it for me.

Pearl: Look! Kongfu Panda is on now.

Ben: Wonderful! Judy, are you all right with that?

Judy: It must be a lot of fun. But look at the crowd. Do you think we'll still be able to get tickets?

Pearl: Come on! We're already here.

Ben: All right! Let's see when the next picture is on.

Judy: Three fifty. There's only 5 minutes left, and look at the long line.

Ben: Shall we take a chance?

Pearl: Yeah, let's try.

Judy: It's moving so slow.

Pearl: We're getting closer … Two more … One more. It's our turn.

Ben: Two tickets, please.

Ticket-Clerk: Will the first row do? The others are all sold out.

Ben: Yes, that's fine.

 Text

Kongfu Panda

Shifu: Master Oogway, you summoned me? Is something wrong?

Master Oogway: Why must something be wrong for me to want to see my old friend?

Shifu: So, nothing is wrong?

Master Oogway: Well, I didn't say that.

Shifu: You were saying?

Master Oogway: I have had a vision. Tai Lung will return.

Shifu: That is impossible. He's in prison.

Master Oogway: Nothing is impossible.

Shifu: Zeng, fly to Chordom Prison. Tell them to double the guards. Double the weapons. Double everything. Tai Lung does not leave that prison.

Zeng: Yes, Master Shifu.

Master Oogway: One often meets his destiny on the road he takes to avoid it.

Shifu: We have to do something. We can't just have him march in the valley. And take his revenge. He'll, he'll…

Master Oogway: Your mind is like this water, my friend. When it is agitated, it becomes difficult to see. But if you allow it to settle, the answer becomes clear.

Shifu: The Dragon's scroll.

Master Oogway: It is time.

Shifu: But who? Who is worthy to be trusted with the secret to limitless power? To become the Dragon Warrior.

Master Oogway: I don't know.

New words

summon /ˈsʌmən/	v.	召唤,传唤,请求,要求
vision /ˈviʒən/	n.	幻觉,幻影,梦想,幻想
return /riˈtəːn/	n.	回,归,返回
impossible /imˈpɔːsəbl/	adj.	不可能的,办不到的
prison /ˈprizn/	n.	监狱
destiny /ˈdestini/	n.	命运
march /mɑːtʃ/	v.	走动,行进
valley /ˈvæli/	n.	山谷,溪谷
revenge /riˈvendʒ/	n.	报仇,报复
agitated /ˈædʒiteitid/	adj.	激动的
settle /ˈsetl/	v.	使(自己)安下心来,使(心情)平静下来,使安宁
scroll /skrəul/	n.	卷轴
limitless /ˈlimitlis/	adj.	无限的,无限制的

扫一扫跟着练

Phrases and expressions

take one's revenge	报仇
be worthy to	值得……

Reading comprehension

Ⅰ. Choose the expression which is the closest in meaning to the underlined part in each sentence.

1. Is something wrong?
    A. Is everything OK?
    B. How's everything going?
    C. What's the matter?

Unit Thirteen　Film

2. Who is worthy to be trusted with the secret to limitless power?
   A. is worthy of being trusted
   B. is worth to be trusted
   C. worth trust

Ⅱ. Answer the questions according to the text.

1. Why does Master Oogway summon Shifu?
_____

2. How does Shifu feel when he learns this?
_____

3. What does Master Oogway tell him?
_____

 Grammar

助动词及其用法

协助主要动词构成谓语动词词组的词叫助动词(Auxiliary Verb)。被协助的动词被称为主要动词(Main Verb)。助动词本身没有词义,不能单独做谓语。它常配合主要动词,协助构成否定句、疑问句、强调句、时态、语态等语法形式。

1. 常见的助动词

常见的助动词包括 be(无词义),do(无词义),have(无词义),shall(将要),will(将要)。助动词自身没有词义,不可单独使用。

例如:

He doesn't like English.

他不喜欢英语。

句中的"doesn't"是助动词,无词义;而"like"是主要动词,有词义。

2. 助动词协助主要动词完成的功用

(1)表示时态,例如:

He is singing.

他在唱歌。

He has got married.

他已结婚。

(2)表示语态,例如:

He was sent to England.

他被派往英国。

(3)构成疑问句,例如:

Do you like college life?

你喜欢大学生活吗?

Did you study English before you came here?

你来这儿之前学过英语吗?

(4)与否定词 not 合用,构成否定句,例如:

I don't like him.

我不喜欢他。

(5)加强语气,例如:

Do come to the party tomorrow evening.

明天晚上一定来参加晚会。

He did know that.

他的确知道那件事。

助动词本身没有词义,不能单独做谓语。它常配合主要动词,协助构成否定句、疑问句、强调句、时态、语态等语法形式。

3. 助动词 be 的用法

be 作为助动词,用来构成进行时态和被动语态。如:

We are working hard in the garden.(构成现在进行时)

我们在花园里辛勤劳动。

The house was painted purple.(构成被动语态)

房子被刷成紫色的。

4. 助动词 do 的用法

do 作为助动词,用来构成疑问句、否定句、强调句。如:

Do you live in Shanghai?(构成疑问句)

你住在上海吗?

I don't like to have hamburgers.(构成否定句)

我不喜欢吃汉堡包。

Do come please.(构成强调句)

一定要来。

5. 助动词 have 的用法

have 作为助动词,用来构成完成时态。如:

Have you finished the work?(构成现在完成时)

你完成工作了没有?

6. 助动词 shall 和 will 的用法

shall 和 will 作为助动词,用来构成将来时态。如:

I will call you this evening.(构成一般将来时)

今晚我会打电话给你。

What shall we do next week?

下个星期我们做什么?

 Fun time

1. While there is life, there is hope.

   一息若存,希望不灭。

• Unit Thirteen　Film

2. You have to believe in yourself. That's the secret of success.
   人必须有自信,这是成功的秘密。

3. Cease to struggle and you cease to live.
   生命不止,奋斗不息。

4. A strong man will struggle with the storms of fate.
   强者能同命运的风暴抗争。

5. Pain past is pleasure.
   过去的痛苦即快乐。

单元复习

I 词汇练习

Fill in each of the gaps with the proper word given below, and change the form where necessary.

　　　revenge　return　valley　impossible　summon　prison　destiny　limitless

1. He _____ his soldiers to fight.
2. We must _____ to Dalian within three days.
3. It's _____ for us to finish the work in one day.
4. The thief was put into _____ for one year.
5. Every spring the river floods the _____ .
6. _____ is sometimes cruel.
7. She said she would take her _____ on Tom.
8. The future holds _____ promise.

II 语法练习

Fill in each of the gaps with the correct form of "be," including the negative form.

1. Where _____ you at 11 o'clock last Friday morning?
2. Don't buy those shoes. They _____ too expensive.
3. Kate got married when she _____ 24 years old.
4. We _____ tired when we arrived home, so we went to bed.
5. What _____ Tim doing when you saw him?
6. We don't like our hotel room. It _____ very small and it _____ very clean.
7. I woke up early yesterday. The sun _____ shining and the birds _____ singing.
8. George _____ at work last week because he _____ ill.
9. You can turn off the radio. I _____ listening to it.
10. "_____ you at home at 9:30 a.m.?" "No, I _____ . I _____ at work."

101

Ⅲ 阅读理解

Read the passage and choose the best choice for each of the questions.

John Jordan is the head of a big shop which sells clothes. He likes to talk to people when they come to do shopping in his shop. His wife, named Mary Jordan, is a teacher, who works in a correspondence school that gives people the opportunity to improve their old skills or to learn new ones. Both John and Mary have to work hard because they need money for their children.

Their son, Mark, is in his first year of a private university which asks for about $10,000 a year. Their daughter, Clare, is now looking after children for busy parents in her spare time so as to make money for her study in the correspondence school where her mother works.

Because taxes are high, food is expensive and prices are going up. It is too expensive for them to buy a nice house. They have to buy a small farm building and change it into a comfortable house for summer.

They put new windows on the sides, which keep the little house cool during the hot summer. They also put in a kitchen, a bathroom and stairs. They put in two small bedrooms on the second floor and another one on the first floor. Their house is well designed.

They all work very hard and love each other. Their life is not rich but very happy.

1. Mr. Jordan is a _____.
   A. doctor　　　　B. lawyer　　　　C. businessman　　D. policeman
2. Mrs. Jordan is now doing a _____.
   A. farm job　　　B. service job　　C. blue collar job　　D. white collar job
3. Clare looks after the children for busy parents because _____.
   A. she loves the children
   B. the busy parents like to share their children with Clare
   C. she needs money to study
   D. her brother doesn't like her
4. They don't buy a nice house just because _____.
   A. Mark doesn't like to study in a private university
   B. John likes to design a new house
   C. Mary wants to live near the correspondence school
   D. it is too expensive for them
5. They feel happy because _____.
   A. they're rich
   B. they work hard and love each other
   C. they seldom go camping
   D. they're going to buy a comfortable house

102

Unit Fourteen　The Olympic Games

Warming up

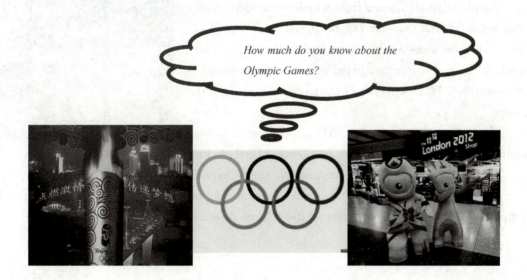

How much do you know about the Olympic Games?

I. Discussion

1. Do you like watching the Olympic Games?
2. How often are the Olympic Games held?
3. When did Beijing succeed in applying for the Olympic Games?
4. What are the names of the five Fuwa?
5. What is the thematic slogan of the Beijing Olympic Games?

II. Pair work: Read the following dialogue with your partner.

A: Do you often have sports at school?
B: Of course. I love sports.
A: Which do you prefer, horse-riding or shooting?
B: Shooting. Do you like shooting?
A: I prefer horse-riding to shooting.
B: What about wrestling and sailing?
A: Both of them are exciting. I like watching them. Are you good at sailing?

B: Yes. In fact, I am on our city team.
A: Great. Would you please let me know when you have a race?
B: Sure.

The Olympic Games

扫一扫跟着练

Every four years athletes from all over the world take part in the Olympic Games. Both the Summer and Winter Olympics are held every four years. The Winter Olympics are usually held two years before the Summer Olympics.

The old Olympic Games from which the modern games came began around the year 776 BC in Greece. Many of the sports were the same as they are now. Some of the games in which the young men competed were: running, jumping and wrestling. Women were not allowed to take part in the games.

After about the year 393 AD the Olympic Games stopped. For centuries there were no Olympic Games. But they were not forgotten.

The first Olympic Games in modern times happened in 1896. They were held in Greece—the country in which the games were born. In the 1896 games there were 311 competitions from just 13 countries. After that more and more countries joined in the games.

New words

扫一扫跟着练

both /bəuθ/	adj.	两……(都), 两个……(都)
around /əˈraund/	adv.	大约
running /ˈrʌniŋ/	n.	奔, 赛跑
jumping /ˈdʒʌmpiŋ/	n.	跳高
wrestling /ˈresliŋ/	n.	摔跤
century /ˈsentʃuri/	n.	世纪, 一百年
modern /ˈmɔdən/	adj.	现代的, 近代的
country /ˈkʌntri/	n.	国家, 国土
born /bɔːn/		(bear 的过去分词) 诞生
competition /ˌkɔmpiˈtiʃən/	n.	比赛, 竞赛, 赛会
join /dʒɔin/	v.	参加, 做……的成员

Unit Fourteen　The Olympic Games

Phrases and expressions

all over the world	世界各地的
take part in	参加,参与(某事物)
allow sb. to do sth.	允许某人做某事
after that	自从那时起

Proper names

the Olympic Games	奥林匹克运动会
Greece	希腊

Reading comprehension

Decide whether the following statements are true（T）or false（F）according to the passage.

(　)1. Both the Summer and Winter Olympics are held every four years.
(　)2. The modern Olympic Games began around the year 776 BC in Greece.
(　)3. The first Olympic Games in modern times were held in 1896.
(　)4. In the 1896 games there were 113 competitions from just 13 countries.
(　)5. Women are not allowed to take part in the games now.

Grammar

并列连词

并列连词主要用来表示并列关系、选择关系、因果推理关系等。
(1)表示并列关系的连词主要含有"和""补充""增加"等意思。常用来表达并列关系的连词有如下几个：

and 和　both…and… 二者都
either…or… 或者……或者……
neither…nor… 既不……也不……
as well as 也,连同
not only…but (also)… 不但……而且……

e.g. I used to live in Paris and London.
我过去住在伦敦和巴黎。
Both Jane and Jim are interested in pop music.
詹妮和吉姆对流行音乐都很感兴趣。
She is not only kind but also honest.

她不但和蔼而且诚实。

Bob as well as his parents is going on holiday this summer.

鲍勃和他的父母今年夏天要去度假。

(2)常用来表示转折关系的并列连词有如下几个：

but 但是

yet 然而

still 仍然

while 然而

e. g. The winter in Peking is very cold while that of Kunming is warm.

北京的冬天很冷，然而昆明的冬天却很温暖。

I explained twice, still he couldn't understand.

我解释了两遍，然而他还不懂。

(3)常用来表示选择关系的并列连词有如下几个：

or (or else) 否则

otherwise 否则

neither…nor… 既不……也不……

either…or… 或者……或者……

e. g. Would you like to leave or would you like to stay?

你是想走还是想留？

You can come either on Saturday or on Sunday.

你可以星期六来，也可以星期天来。

Neither you nor I nor anyone else believes such a thing.

不管你、我或者其他任何人都不会相信这样一件事。

(4)常用来表示因果推理关系的并列连词主要有 so, for, then, therefore 等。

e. g. The air here is polluted, so the crops are dying.

这里的空气受到了污染，所以庄稼快死了。

The leaves of the trees are falling, for it's already autumn.

树叶在落下，因为秋天已经到来了。

Fun time

1. Nothing venture, nothing have.
   不入虎穴，焉得虎子。

2. One flower makes no garland.
   一朵鲜花难成花环。

3. One today is worth two tomorrows.
   今日一天胜似明日两天。

4. Pleasing ware is half sold.
   商品好看，等于卖出一半。

Unit Fourteen   The Olympic Games

5. Prevention is better than cure.
   预防胜于治疗。

单元复习

I 词汇练习

Fill in each of the gaps with the proper word given below, and change the form where necessary.

both   join   around   century   running   country   competition   modern

1. _____ his eyes were severely burned.
2. The journey will take _____ ten days.
3. He practises _____ every morning.
4. We live in the twentieth _____.
5. In the afternoon they went to an exhibition of _____ art.
6. I entered a chess _____ and finished third.
7. He didn't know much about foreign _____.
8. I'll persuade him to _____ our club.

II 语法练习

Choose the best answer for each of the sentences from the four choices below.

1. My aunt asks whether I like a woolen sweater _____ a cotton one.
   A. but   B. or   C. and   D. not
2. Be quick, _____ we'll be late.
   A. and   B. or   C. but   D. so
3. We ran to the trees, _____ we couldn't see any more monkeys.
   A. but   B. so   C. and   D. for
4. You can _____ stay at home _____ go out to play.
   A. either; or   B. so; that   C. neither; and   D. both; and
5. _____ Monday _____ Tuesday is OK, I will be free then.
   A. Either; or   B. Neither; nor   C. So; that   D. Both; and
6. _____ my brother _____ my sister are doctors.
   A. Not; but   B. Neither; nor   C. Both; and   D. Either; or
7. You may sit _____ this end _____ that end of the boat.
   A. neither; nor   B. both; and   C. either; or   D. between; and
8. None of the shoes are the right size. They are _____ too big _____ too small.
   A. or; or   B. either; or   C. neither; or   D. both; and

107

9. We went _____ to the cinema, _____ to the park.
   A. did not; /   B. not; but   C. either; or   D. both; and
10. Last week we saw _____ Li Ming _____ Mary.
    A. neither; or   B. either; nor   C. all; and   D. not; but

Ⅲ 阅读理解

Read the passage and choose the best answer for each of the gaps from the four choices.

China is already the world's third largest producer of electronics, and becoming a player in the global appliance market. Twenty years ago, U.S., European and Japanese companies started moving into China to supply the local market with household goods. Now those same companies are getting whipped by Chinese competitors. Over the past six years, the market share of foreign TV makers in China has dropped from 70 percent to less than 20 percent. Matsushita opened the first microwave-oven plant in China in 1995. Two years later the Chinese company Galanz started making microwaves and selling them for half Matsushita's price.

Chinese companies now make more than 43 million TVs yearly. Konka, one of China's largest TV makers, sells its branded TVs in the United States, and has set up factories in Mexico to service the American market, while TCL, another major TV maker, exported 11 million units from its Chinese factories last year. It has more Southeast Asian factories than any other Chinese company.

1. This passage is primarily concerned with _____.
   A. the world's third largest producer of electronics
   B. Chinese electronic companies
   C. China's largest TV makers
   D. the increase of China's electronics
2. What do "whipped" mean?
   A. Beat with a whip.   B. Won.
   C. Defeated.   D. Suffered.
3. What is the decreased rate of the market share of foreign TV makers in China?
   A. 70%.   B. 20%.
   C. 50%.   D. 20%~70%.
4. When did Galanz start making and selling microwaves?
   A. 1993.   B. 1994.
   C. 1995.   D. 1997.
5. Which of the following produces more TV sets?
   A. Galanz.   B. Konka.
   C. TCL.   D. Unknown.

Unit Fifteen   Health

 Warming up

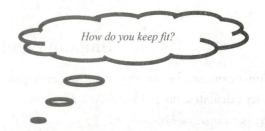

How do you keep fit?

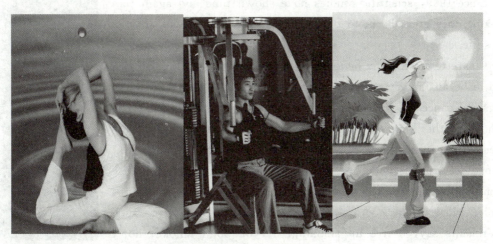

Ⅰ. **Discussion**

1. Do you like sports?
2. Do you often exercise for your health?
3. Do you often take part in activities that are bad for your health?
4. Do you often eat food that is bad for your health?
5. Is it good for people to try to lose weight?

Ⅱ. **Pair work: Read the following dialogue with your partner.**

Mike: Look at those men on TV! What should I do to keep myself in shape, John?

John: Just look around you, Mike. Look at me, for example.

Mike: I am looking at you. You don't lift weights. You don't go to any fitness club.

John: No. But I go jogging regularly. And look at Lisa. She plays badminton and her brother is crazy about playing basketball.

Mike: How about Ben?

John: He's a couch potato, just like you.

Mike: But he doesn't look so bad, does he?

John: Well, he always works so hard. But whenever he has free time, he will watch TV rather than exercise. So he often has a backache. Do you want to end up like that?

Mike: OK. Well…

John: Come on! I would get up right now and throw away those chips if I were you.

Smoking and Health

Americans smoke six thousand million cigarettes every year. It has been calculated that 51% of American men smoke while 34% of American women do so.

Since 1939, scientific studies have shown time and again that smoking does great harm to one's health and that it will shorten one's life.

Cigarette smoking is believed by most research workers in this field to be an important cause in the development of cancer of the lungs and cancer of the throat and is believed to have much to do with some other kinds of cancers. Cigarette smokers suffer from the illness of the heart more often than those who don't smoke. But strange yet true, women are thought to be less affected, because when women smoke, they usually don't breathe in the smoke so deeply. Most of the doctors and researchers who have done such experiments say, "Give up smoking. If you don't smoke—don't start!"

Filters are required now to make smoking a bit safer, but they can only reduce, not get rid of its poison.

Of course there are still a number of doctors and researchers who are less sure of the effect of cigarette smoking on health. They believe that cancers of the lungs, the throat and so on may also be caused by atmosphere pollution, or chemical poison that is now being used by farmers in large quantities to destroy plant pests and small animals.

Unit Fifteen Health

扫一扫跟着练

New words

smoke /sməuk/	v.	抽烟,吸烟
cigarette /ˌsigəˈret/	n.	香烟
calculate /ˈkælkjuˌleit/	v.	计算
research /riˈsəːtʃ/	n.	研究,调查
field /fiːld/	n.	领域
cause /kɔːz/	n.	原因,理由
development /diˈveləpmənt/	n.	发展,进展,发生,成长
cancer /ˈkænsə/	n.	癌,毒瘤
throat /θrəut/	n.	喉咙,咽喉
suffer /ˈsʌfə/	v.	受痛苦,受损害
affect /əˈfekt/	v.	影响,感动
deeply /ˈdiːpli/	adv.	深深地
experiment /iksˈperimənt/	n.	实验,试验
prove /pruːv/	v.	证明,证实,检验,考验
satisfaction /ˌsætisˈfækʃən/	n.	满意,满足,满意的事情
filter /ˈfiltə/	n.	(香烟的)过滤嘴
require /riˈkwaiə/	v.	要求,需求,命令
poison /ˈpɔizn/	n.	毒药,毒害
atmosphere /ˈætməsfiə/	n.	空气,大气
chemical /ˈkemikəl/	adj.	化学的
pest /pest/	n.	害虫,有害动物

Phrases and expressions

time and again	反复地
do harm to	危害……,伤害……
shorten one's life	缩短寿命
have much to do with	与……有很大关系
suffer from	忍受,遭受
breathe in	吸入
give up	放弃
a bit	一点儿
get rid of	摆脱,除掉,去掉
a number of	许多,一些
in large quantities	大量地

Reading comprehension

Choose the one that best completes each of the following statements according to the text.

1. In America, _____ smoke cigarettes.
   A. 34% of men and 51% of women
   B. 51% of men and 34% of women
   C. six thousand million men

2. According to the second paragraph, _____.
   A. smoking is not bad for the health of human beings
   B. smoking is rather harmful to the health of human beings
   C. smoking is helpful to human beings

3. Which of the following is not true?
   A. Smoking can cause cancers of the lungs, the throat and so on.
   B. Male smokers are thought to be less affected than female smokers.
   C. Filters can not get rid of the poison from the cigarettes.

4. Filters are useful in _____.
   A. reducing the poison from the cigarettes
   B. getting rid of the poison from the cigarettes
   C. making smoking quite safe

5. According to the last paragraph, some doctors and researchers believe that _____.
   A. smoking does great harm to one's health
   B. smoking is good for one's health
   C. besides smoking, there are other causes in the development of cancers.

Grammar

状语从句

一、if 引导的条件状语从句

引导条件状语从句最常用的连词是 if。常见的 if 条件状语从句表示在某条件下,某事很可能发生,条件是可能存在的,主句中某种情况发生的概率也是很高的。如:

If you ask him, he will help you.
如果你请他帮忙,他会帮你的。

If you fail in the exam, you will let him down.
如果你考试不及格,你会让他失望的。

If you have finished the homework, you can go home.
如果你做完了作业,就可以回家了。

另外,if 从句还表示不可实现的条件或根本不可能存在的条件,也就是一种虚拟的条件或

假设。从句多用一般过去时或过去完成时,表示对现在或过去的一种假设。如:

If I were you, I would invite him to the party.

如果我是你,我会邀请他参加聚会。

I would have arrived much earlier if I had not been caught in the traffic.

要不是交通堵塞,我本来会来得早一些。

二、when 引导的时间状语从句

when 是引导时间状语从句最常用的一个词,它涵盖的时间范围比较广泛,在作"当……的时候"解时,有下面几种常见用法。

(1)表示在某个具体的时间点发生的动作。此时,when 不能用 as 或 while 替换。

When she comes, I shall tell her to wait for you.

她来的时候我会告诉她等你的。(指具体的时间点)

When his father died of illness in 1980, he was only two years old.

1980 年他父亲病逝时他只有两岁。(指 1980 年这个具体的时间点)

(2)表示一个动作与另一个动作在同一时间发生,或一个动作在另一个动作所延续的时间范围之内发生。此时,when 可以用 as 或 while 替换。

I hurt my shoulder when (while, as) I was playing basketball.

我打篮球时弄伤了肩膀。

When (While, As) Tom was reading, Jim was writing.

汤姆看书的时候,吉姆在写东西。

两个同时发生的动作,如果不是一次性而是重复性的,即过去或现在的习惯动作,可用连词 when 或 whenever,意思是"每当……的时候"。

例如:

When (Whenever) he goes to town, he always visits his aunt.

每当他去镇上,他都去拜访他姑姑。

She always felt ill when (whenever) she ate oyster.

她每次吃牡蛎都会生病。

在上述两例中,不管是用 when 还是用 whenever,主句动词和从句动词或者都用一般现在时,或者都用一般过去时,分别表示现在或过去的习惯动作。

(3)表示从句的动作发生后,主句的动作立即发生。此时,when 表示动作的先后顺序,相当于 after,不能用 as 或 while 替换。

When he had done his homework, he watched television.

=After he had done his homework, he watched television.

他做完作业后看电视。

When he had painted the windows, he painted the doors.

=After he had painted the windows, he painted the doors.

他把窗户油漆完后,又把门油漆了。

在这里,when 从句的谓语动词都用了完成时态,when 从句既可以置于句首,也可以置于句尾。

Fun time

1. Man struggles upwards; water flows downwards.
   人往高处走,水往低处流。
2. Out of sight, out of mind.
   眼不见,心不烦。
3. Practice makes perfect.
   熟能生巧。
4. Sense comes with age.
   老马识途。
5. Every advantage has its disadvantage.
   有利必有弊。

单元复习

I 词汇练习

Choose the best choice for each of the gaps.

1. The scientists are able to _____ accurately when the spaceship will reach the moon.
   A. calculate   B. hope   C. guess
2. I met her _____ I was at school.
   A. as   B. if   C. while
3. She likes dogs, _____ does he.
   A. so   B. either   C. as
4. Did the storm _____ any harm to the corn?
   A. have   B. take   C. do
5. His parents have many friends in the _____ of politics.
   A. field   B. land   C. piece
6. You have no _____ to be anxious, I think.
   A. causing   B. cause   C. idea
7. The driver has much to do _____ that serious accident.
   A. with   B. in   C. over
8. She was suffering _____ a headache at that time.
   A. with   B. from   C. by
9. There is much _____ difficulty than I thought. So I think we can finish it earlier.
   A. fewer   B. less   C. more

10. They are not _____ poor as they once were.
   A. so   B. such   C. that
11. My father has _____ smoking since he got lung cancer.
   A. given in   B. given up   C. given on
12. Are you sure _____ the effect of this?
   A. in   B. with   C. of

II 语法练习

Complete each of the following sentences with the conjunction of "when" or "if."

1. _____ you know someone very well, you may just say "Hello" as a greeting.
2. _____ he was born, his family lived in the countryside.
3. _____ I came back home, Mum was cooking.
4. _____ it is fine tomorrow, we can go to the zoo.
5. _____ I first used the machine, I pressed the wrong button.
6. _____ you need more help, please let me know.
7. _____ you ask him, he will help you.
8. _____ you fail in the exam, you will let him down.
9. _____ I saw her, she was typing a letter.
10. _____ you have finished the homework, you can go home.

III 阅读理解

Read the passage and choose the best answer for each of the questions below.

Mr. and Mrs. Williams had always spent their summer holidays in England in the past, in a small hotel at the seaside. One year, however, Mr. Williams made a lot of money in his business, so they decided to go to Rome and stay at a really good hotel while they went around that famous city.

They flew to Rome, and arrived at their hotel late one evening. They expected that they would have to go to bed hungry, because in the small hotel they had been used to in the past, there was no food after seven o'clock in the evening. They were surprised when the clerk who received them in the hotel asked them whether they would be taking dinner there that night.

"Are you still serving dinner then?" asked Mrs. Williams.

"Yes, certainly, madam," answered the clerk. "We serve it until half past nine."

"What are the times of meals then?" asked Mr. Williams.

"Well, sir," answered the clerk, "we serve breakfast from seven to half-past eleven in the morning, lunch from twelve to three in the afternoon, tea from four to five, and dinner from six to half past nine."

"But that hardly leaves any time for us to travel around Rome!" said Mrs. Williams in a disappointed voice.

1. Did Mr. and Mrs. Williams use to stay in a small hotel in England for their summer holidays?

    A. Yes.   B No.   C. Doesn't say.

2. Did they decide to spend their summer holidays in Rome one year?

    A. Yes.   B No.   C. Doesn't say.

3. Did they go to Rome by train?

    A. Yes.   B. No.   C. Doesn't say.

4. Did they have to go hungry when they arrived at their hotel late that evening?

    A. Yes.   B. No.   C. Doesn't say.

5. Would they go back home immediately because they didn't have any time to travel around Rome?

    A. Yes.   B. No.   C. Doesn't say.

Unit Sixteen   Pollution

Warming up

Are you suffering from pollution?

I. Discussion

1. Is pollution one of the serious problems we face?
2. Is industry to blame for some of the pollution we are suffering from?
3. Are factories and oil tankers sources of water pollution?
4. Are factories and cars the major sources of air pollution in your hometown?
5. Have measures been taken in your neighbourhood to stop pollution?

II. Pair work: Read the following dialogue with your partner.

Robert: Dad, how foggy it is this morning!

Mr. Brown: Yes, it's a new problem.

Robert: A new problem? Why do you say so?

Mr. Brown: The problem results from smog.

Robert: Smog? What is it?

Mr. Brown: The word "smog" is a blend of two words: "smoke" and "fog." Smog has affected people more than any other type of air pollution.

Robert: I see. Look, there are some plastic bags floating on the river.

Mr. Brown: Some citizens are still ignorant of environmental protection. It's really a pity!

Robert: But, anyway, public concern over environmental pollution has greatly increased. There is hope for the future.

Pollution

Pollution means the poisoning of the land, the seas and the air. It is one of the greatest problems facing mankind today. Industry is to blame for some of the pollution that exists. Some factory chimneys release dangerous fumes, smoke and dust into the air. Factory wastes containing dangerous chemicals are sometimes poured directly into our rivers without being treated. The amounts released at any one time may be small, but they can build up over a period of time and cause real harm to human beings and wildlife.

Water pollution is serious because we all rely on a supply of pure water to live. River pollution can become so bad that fish and plants cannot live. In some countries, local governments add to the pollution problem by allowing untreated wastes to flow into the rivers and seas. Oil is increasing pollution at sea. A tanker may discharge oil by accident, or on purpose when its tanks are being cleaned out. Oil pollutes beaches and kills seabirds.

In most developed countries, fumes from cars are a major cause of air pollution. Cars give out poisonous gases. In cities these gases can build up to dangerous levels at times.

We use insecticides to kill insects that attack crops. In doing so, we may upset the balance of nature by killing the food supply for birds. In some cases, the substances in insecticides may also harm animals that feed on the crops.

Over the last few years, people throughout the world have realized the dangers of pollution. At last, international action is being taken. Most governments have passed anti-pollution laws. Factories are ordered to remove the poisons from their wastes before discharging them into the air or the rivers. Already, in some countries, the air is cleaner, and the rivers are beginning to support fish and plant life again.

blame /bleim/   v.   责备, 谴责
chimney /ˈtʃimni/   n.   烟囱

• Unit Sixteen   Pollution

fume /fju:m/	n.	烟气
dust /dʌst/	n.	灰尘
harm /hɑ:m/	n.	伤害,损害
rely /ri'lai/	v.	依靠
pure /pjuə/	adj.	纯的,纯净的
untreated /ʌn'tri:tid/	adj.	未经处理的
waste /weist/	n.	浪费,废物
flow /fləu/	v.	流,流动
tanker /'tæŋkə/	n.	油轮
discharge /dis'tʃɑ:dʒ/	v.	排放,排出
tank /tæŋk/	n.	大容器,仓,柜
pollute /pə'lu:t/	v.	污染
seabird /'si:bə:d/	n.	海鸟
level /'levl/	n.	水平
insecticide /in'sektisaid/	n.	杀虫剂
upset /ʌp'set/	v.	弄翻,打乱
balance /'bæləns/	n.	平衡
case /keis/	n.	情况,事情
substance /'sʌbstəns/	n.	物质
anti-pollution /'æntipə'lu:ʃn/	n.	反污染
remove /ri'mu:v/	v.	移动,搬开,去掉

Phrases and expressions

build up	增大,集结
at times	有时
developed countries	发达国家
by accident	偶然地
on purpose	故意地,有意地
rely on	依靠,指望,信任

Reading comprehension

Choose the one that best completes each of the following statements according to the text.

1. Factories may cause _____.
    A. both air and water pollution
    B. only air pollution
    C. only water pollution

2. _____ may result from those factories that discharge into the rivers wastes containing poisonous chemicals.
    A. Air pollution

119

B. Water pollution

C. Air and water pollution

3. Water pollution is dangerous because _____ great harm to us.

   A. polluted sea water does

   B. the dead seabirds do

   C. polluted drinking water and sea food do

4. In cities in developed countries _____ may be a major cause of air pollution.

   A. smoke from restaurants

   B. poisonous gases from cars

   C. wastes containing harmful chemicals

5. In the world _____ pollution.

   A. people are fighting against

   B. governments are no longer unaware of the danger of

   C. factories have stopped discharging wastes so that they are no longer causes of

6. Pollution has come under better control _____.

   A. in most countries

   B. at least in some countries

   C. in some countries where industry is not highly developed

 Grammar

从属连词引导状语从句

从属连词(subordinate conjunctions)可以用来引导状语从句。

1. 从属连词引导目的状语从句

引导目的状语从句的连词主要有下面这些：

(1) in order that：

He left early in order that his children would not be alone in the house.

他早早动身，以免孩子们单独待在家里。

I lent him ￥500 in order(so)that he might go for a holiday.

我借给他500元，以便他能去度假。

(2) so that：

Ask her to hurry up with the letters so that I can sign them.

让她快点把信打好，以便我能签字。

Please interpret this Chinese woman's remarks so that I can understand them.

请翻译一下这位中国妇女的话，以便我能听懂。

(3) so：

Can't you fix it somehow so you could stay longer?

难道你不能做某种安排以便能多待些日子？

I'll give him a map so he won't get lost.

Unit Sixteen　Pollution

我会给他一张地图免得他迷路。

（4）that：

She did it that he might go free.

她这样做以便他能获得自由。

I am anxious to get done that I may be back in Ireland.

我急于完成此事以便能返回爱尔兰。

（5）lest：

He hurried on, lest she should meet him again.

他赶紧往前走,唯恐她再碰到他。

He hid the money lest it should be stolen.

他把钱藏起来唯恐别人偷去。

2. 从属连词引导结果状语从句

结果状语从句主要由 so…that 和 such…that 引导。

（1）so…that：

He was so young that you must excuse him.

他那样年轻,你得原谅他。

He was so fat that he couldn't get through the door.

他胖得连门都过不去了。

（2）such…that：

Jim made such a noise that his sister told him to be quiet.

吉姆吵成那样,他姐姐让他安静点。

He shut the window with such force that the glass broke.

他关窗时那样使劲,连玻璃都震碎了。

They had such a fierce dog that no one dared to go near their house.

他们的狗那样凶,谁也不敢走近他们家。

3. so that 也可以引导结果状语从句

so that 引导的是目的状语从句还是引导结果状语从句,除根据上下文意义判定外,还可以从结构上分辨。so that 之前有逗号则通常为结果状语；如没有逗号,则看从句中有没有情态动词,如果有,多半为目的状语,否则多半为结果状语。

We all arrived at 8, so that the meeting began in time. （结果）

Let's start early so that we can get there in time. （目的）

Turn on the light so that we may see it clearly . （目的）

He turned the light on so that I saw it clearly . （结果）

 Fun time

1. Custom makes all things easy.
   习惯成自然。

2. Do not pull all your eggs in one basket.
   别把所有的蛋都放在一个篮子里。

3. East or west, home is the best.
   东奔西跑,还是家里好。
4. Experience is the best teacher.
   实践出真知。
5. Faith can move mountains.
   精诚所至,金石为开。

单元复习

I 词汇练习

Fill in each of the gaps with the proper word given below, and change the form where necessary.

remove   level   flow   pour   upset   pollute   blame   local   rely   balance

1. He _____ from one bedroom into another.
2. Never drink _____ water. It may harm your health.
3. Don't _____ on him for help. He is not interested in the work.
4. Most of the rivers in China _____ from the west to the east.
5. She _____ wine into each of the 5 glasses.
6. He was suddenly ill, which _____ my plan to work with him.
7. He works in the _____ court.
8. We must increase production _____.
9. The driver was not to _____ for the accident.
10. The girl lost her _____ and fell off the balance beam.

II 语法练习

Choose for each of the sentences the best answer from the four given below.

1. We love spring _____ there're beautiful flowers everywhere.
   A. but   B. if
   C. though   D. because
2. I'll tell him to give you a call _____ he comes back.
   A. because   B. since
   C. as soon as   D. but
3. You should finish your exercises _____ you go to bed.
   A. after   B. before   C. because   D. if
4. Mr. Smith has taught in that small town _____ he left Canada in 1988.
   A. when   B. after   C. for   D. since

• Unit Sixteen　Pollution

5. You'll do better in English _____ you work harder.
   A. or   B. than
   C. if   D. before
6. Tom didn't go to school yesterday _____ he was ill.
   A. but   B. until
   C. if   D. because
7. What shall we do _____ it rains tomorrow?
   A. so   B. if
   C. but   D. because
8. The room is _____ dirty _____ we don't want to stay here.
   A. so, that   B. such, that
   C. either, or   D. as, as
9. _____ she is young, she knows quite a lot.
   A. When   B. However
   C. Although   D. Unless
10. —Would you like to come to dinner tonight?
    —I'd like to, _____ I'm too busy.
    A. and   B. so
    C. as   D. but

Ⅲ　阅读理解

Read the passage and choose the best answer for each of the questions.

One Thursday evening Mr. Smith left his car in front of his house as usual, but when he came down the next morning to go to his office, he found that his car was missing. He called the police and told them what had happened, and they said they would try to find the car for him.

When Mr. Smith came back from his office that evening, the car was in the usual place outside the home. He examined it carefully to see whether it was broken and found two tickets on one of the seats, and a letter which said, "We are sorry we took your car because of something important." Mr. and Mrs. Smith went to the theater with the two tickets the next evening and they had a good time.

When they got home, they found that thieves had taken almost everything they had in their home.

1. Mr. Smith usually _____.
   A. went away from his car on Thursday night
   B. stayed in his car until it was night
   C. went to and came back from work in his car
   D. didn't get out of his car until the next morning

2. Mr. Smith called the police _____.
   A. to tell them who had stolen his car
   B. to ask them what had happened
   C. to ask them for the car
   D. to ask them to help find the car
3. When was the car stolen?
   A. At night.
   B. In the morning.
   C. In the afternoon.
   D. When Mr. Smith was not at home.
4. Who sent back the car?
   A. The police.   B. The thieves.
   C. Smith's friends.   D. Mrs. Smith.
5. On _____ Mr. and Mrs. Smith went to the theatre with the two tickets.
   A. Saturday night   B. Sunday night
   C. Wednesday night   D. Monday night

Unit Seventeen News

Warming up

How do you get the information you need?

Ⅰ. **Discussion**

1. Do you often read news?
2. What kind of news do you like best?
3. What are the different ways people get news?
4. Do you think children like (= are interested in) the news?（Why？/Why not？）
5. How does the news affect people?

Ⅱ. **Pair work：Read the following dialogue with your partner.**

A：It is a bit windy, isn't it?

B：It is a bit. But I don't mind the wind.

A：It is better than last week. It snowed so much last week.

B：I wonder what it's going to be like tomorrow.

A：You are going to ride up the CN Tower(加拿大国家电视塔), aren't you?

B：Yes, if the weather is fine. You know, on a clear day, one can see the mist from Niagara Falls.

A: Is Diana going with you or is she going to visit her friends tomorrow?

B: She is not going with me. The idea of riding in a glass lift is too much for her.

A: She said she'd love to go up, didn't she?

B: Well, she changed her mind. She will go and buy some more winter clothes tomorrow.

A: Look, black clouds are coming. It may snow again. You aren't going to forget about the CN Tower, are you?

A News Report

Here is the news:

A mother and a child died this morning because of a storm. They lived in a small house near Bridge Road. The house was in poor condition. Last night, strong winds blew and the rain kept pouring down. Didn't the owner do anything? Yes, he called the police for help. But the road was bad and it took the police an hour and a half to get to the house. The house collapsed before they arrived. Only the father and a three-year-old boy managed to get out.

The weather forecast calls for rain tonight and the temperature may drop about 10 degrees. The mayor is warning everyone not to stay in dangerous houses.

New words

news /njuːz/	n.	新闻,消息,报道
die /dai/	v.	死
storm /stɔːm/	n.	暴风雨
condition /kənˈdiʃən/	n.	条件
rain /rein/	n.	雨,雨水
police /pəˈliːs/	n.	警察,警方
collapse /kəˈlæps/	v.	倒塌
weather /ˈweðə/	n.	天气
temperature /ˈtempritʃə/	n.	温度,气温
dangerous /ˈdeindʒərəs/	adj.	危险的,不安全的,招致危险的

• Unit Seventeen　News

Phrases and expressions

because of	因为
Bridge Road	大桥路
last night	昨晚
call … for help	打电话求助于……
an hour and a half	一个半小时
three-year-old	3 岁的

Reading comprehension

Answer the following questions according to the text.

1. Who died this morning?

   _____

2. What was the weather like last night?

   _____

3. Did it take long for the police to get there?

   _____

4. What will the temperature be like tonight?

   _____

5. What is the mayor telling people?

   _____

Grammar

复合不定代词的用法

复合不定代词是由 some,any,no,every 和 body,thing,one 构成的合成词。

(1)自身的意义以及对句式的要求:构成复合不定代词的两个部分分别表示不同的意义和对句式的要求以及考虑其表人还是表物。

body 用来表人,thing 用来表物,one 既可表人也可表物。

some 表示"某",用于肯定陈述句或用情态动词引导的问句中。

any 表示"某",用于否定句或问句。

no 表示"没有",用于肯定句说明否定意义。

every 表示"每一",用于肯定句或问句。

(2)主谓一致性关系:复合不定代词任何时候都被视为单数,做主语时,谓语动词使用第三人称单数形式。例如:

错:Everybody in our class are interested in English.

对：Everybody in our class is interested in English.

（3）定语后置关系：对复合不定代词进行修饰的词语必须后置，即放在它的后面。例如：

错：I have important something to tell you.

对：I have something important to tell you.

（4）none 和其他复合不定代词在用法上的区别：none 在句中不能单独做主语，但可同 of 连用，后接名词一起做主语；其他复合不定代词可单独做主语，但不能同 of 连用。例如：

错：He is new here, so none knows him.

对：He is new here, so no one knows him.

错：Nobody of them has been to England before.

对：None of them has been to England before.

（5）代换复合不定代词的人称代词：在使用人称代词代换复合不定代词时，应考虑其表人还是表物，即表人时，用 they 代换；而表物时，用 it 代换。例如：

Something is wrong with your computer, isn't it?

Nobody has been there before, have they?

 Fun time

1. Never give advice unasked.
   别人不求助，切莫提忠告。
2. Never judge from appearances.
   人不可貌相。
3. Never look at a gift horse in the mouth.
   对待礼物切莫挑剔。
4. Never swap horses in midstream.
   行到河中不换马。
5. Nobody's enemy but his own.
   不要自寻烦恼。

单元复习

I 词汇练习

Fill in each of the gaps with the proper word, and change the form where necessary.

      temperature   news   condition   died   rain
      weather   collapse   police   dangerous   storm

1. The _____ dropped abruptly.
2. Shooting off firecrackers can be _____.

Unit Seventeen　News

3. A few days later he told me an exciting piece of ＿＿＿＿．
4. He ＿＿＿＿ in battle.
5. The ship had no sooner dropped anchor than a ＿＿＿＿ broke.
6. The miners there worked in dreadful ＿＿＿＿．
7. Do you get much ＿＿＿＿？
8. We must inform the ＿＿＿＿．
9. Having been neglected for years, the house ＿＿＿＿．
10. Whether we will go picnicking tomorrow depends on the ＿＿＿＿．

II 语法练习

Fill in each of the gaps with somebody, anybody, anything or nobody.

1. ＿＿＿＿ broke the window last night.
2. Did ＿＿＿＿ see or hear ＿＿＿＿？
3. I didn't hear or see ＿＿＿＿．
4. I heard a big noise and I looked out, but I didn't see ＿＿＿＿．
5. —I heard a noise outside last night. There was a strong wind. I think the window wasn't closed. It broke in the wind.
   —I think you are right. ＿＿＿＿ broke it. It was the wind.
6. He mistook me for ＿＿＿＿ else.
7. I've called but ＿＿＿＿ answered.
8. He didn't want to team up with ＿＿＿＿．

III 阅读理解

Read the passage and choose the best answer for each of the questions from the four given below.

China's central authorities have outlined a series of new guidelines on improving the country's market economic mechanism. These measures are contained in a communiqué issued on Tuesday at the end of a plenary session of the Chinese Communist Party's Central Committee(CCPCC).

One way of doing so is to perfect a market economy of public, collective and private ownership, with public ownership still as the main pillar. But the communiqué also stipulates that the share-holding system should be the main form in realizing public ownership so as to revitalize the state sector. Private capital will be allowed in infrastructure construction. Another step is to build an integrated nationwide market to encourage the free flow of capital and commodities. During the four-day meeting, more than 300 Central Committee members and alternative members examined and approved a work report by the Political Bureau on its work during the past year.

They also approved a draft proposal with regard to amendments to the state constitution.

1. What does "communiqué" in the 1st passage probably mean?

   A. Commune.

   B. Communication.

   C. Official report to the public.

   D. Declaration or statement.

2. According to the 2nd paragraph, "doing so" may refer to _____.

   A. outlining a series of new guidelines

   B. improving the country's market economic mechanism

   C. containing measures in a communiqué

   D. issuing it on Tuesday

3. According to the passage, which of the following is the major force in a market economy?

   A. Public ownership.

   B. Collective and private ownership.

   C. Share-holding system.

   D. Private capital.

4. On what day of the week did the meeting convene?

   A. On Tuesday.

   B. Four days ago.

   C. On Saturday.

   D. On Friday.

5. Which of the following is the best title of the passage?

   A. A series of new guidelines.

   B. The plenary session of CCPCC.

   C. A gist of the communiqué.

   D. The four-day meeting of CCPCC.

Unit Eighteen   Advertising

 Warming up

Do you know the trade marks in the pictures?

Ⅰ. Discussion

1. Do you believe what is usually said in advertisements?
2. Does advertising affect your behaviour?
3. Have you been fooled by an advertisement?
4. Are you interested in advertisements?
5. Do you think that most advertisements are well done?

Ⅱ. Pair work: Read the following dialogue with your partner.

Jack: What's the matter with you?

Mary: I'm so angry. You won't believe it if I tell you.

Jack: What happened?

Mary: You know, I saw this advertisement in a newspaper. The company is selling an exercise machine called "Beauty."

Jack: Beauty, haha.

Mary: The advertisement says that the machine will make you a beauty in one week. And it also says it's good for all people, easy to use, and the quality is good.

Jack: Don't trust advertisements. They always tell lies. They use beautiful words and all those film stars to fool you. I never believe them.

Mary: Well, when I received the machine, I found there were many things wrong with it.

Jack: That's too bad. Did you call them and ask for your money back?

Mary: Yes, I did. But the company wouldn't do it. They just said they could send people to my home and repair it for me.

Jack: Repair? But it's a new one. They should replace it with a new one.

Mary: But I don't want it any more. I can't trust them anymore. They should give all my money back.

Jack: Did they agree?

Mary: No, they said I hadn't used it properly. They don't even want to replace it for me.

Jack: Oh, that's unbelievable. You should call 315 and I'm sure you can get the money back.

Mary: That's what my parents told me to do, too. I think I will do it.

Jack: Next time don't trust an advertisement so easily. Use your head.

Mary: Not all advertisements are bad, but I will be careful for sure.

Jack: Good for you!

Advertisements

Advertisements are part of our everyday lives. We meet them in newspapers, on the radio and television, in the street and even in buses and trains. We are so used to them that it would be very strange to wake up one morning and find that they have all disappeared.

Yet advertising by manufacturers only occurs on a large scale in certain countries, where enterprise leads to competition and competition to advertisement. But in some other countries where the state controls production, there is no great competition but equally there are very few brand names and only a limited choice of articles. Under these circumstances, most of the brand names are naturally well-known. If there is, for instance, only one brand of tooth-paste, it is pointless to advertise it.

On the other hand, people often feel that competing manufacturers spend so much

Unit Eighteen Advertising

money on advertising their various brands that they have to increase the prices of their articles. But although a lot of money is spent on advertising, this only raises the selling price of each mass-produced article by a very little amount.

And from the manufacturers' point of view, such a small amount would not affect their sales.

Even though advertisements are the result of competition, they do have a useful function: that of giving information. Of course, people often complain that advertisements misinform rather than inform. But do any of us actually believe all we are told in an advertisement?

New words

扫一扫跟着练

advertisement /əd'vɜːtismənt/	n.	广告
radio /'reidiəu/	n.	无线电,收音机
television /'teliˌviʒən/	n.	电视
advertising /'ædvəˌtaiziŋ/	n.	广告业,广告
manufacturer /ˌmænju'fæktʃərə/	n.	制造业者,厂商
occur /ə'kə/	v.	发生,出现
scale /skeil/	n.	规模
enterprise /'entəpraiz/	n.	企业,创业
competition /ˌkɔmpi'tiʃən/	n.	竞争,竞赛
production /prə'dʌkʃən/	n.	生产,产出
equally /'iːkwəli/	adv.	相等地,平等地,同样地
brand /brænd/	n.	商标,牌子
limited /'limitid/	adj.	有限的
choice /tʃɔis/	n.	选择,选择机会,选择权
article /'ɑːtikl/	n.	物品,商品
circumstance /'sɜːkəmstəns/	n.	情况
naturally /'nætʃərəli/	adv.	自然地
tooth-paste /tuːθ peist/	n.	牙膏
pointless /'pɔintlis/	adj.	无意义的
advertise /'ædvətaiz/	v.	做广告,登广告
various /'vɛəriəs/	adj.	不同的,多种多样的
raise /reiz/	v.	提高,升起
mass-produced /mæsprə'djuːst/	adj.	大量生产的
function /'fʌŋkʃən/	n.	功能,作用
complain /kəm'plein/	v.	抱怨,埋怨
misinform /'misin'fɔːm/	v.	告诉……错误的消息

133

Phrases and expressions

wake up	醒来
on a large scale	大规模地，大量地
lead to sth.	导致，引起，通往
under these circumstances	在这些条件下，在这些情况下
most of	大部分的，大多数的
spend … on	在……方面花费……
from sb. 's point of view	从某人的观点看
even though	即使，虽然
rather than	而不是

 Reading comprehension

Choose the one that best completes each of the following statements according to the text.

1. The first paragraph tells us that advertisements _____.

    A. are quite popular in modern society

    B. usually occur on the radio and television

    C. will disappear when you wake up one morning

2. According to the second paragraph, advertising occurs because _____.

    A. the state controls production

    B. there is competition among enterprises

    C. it is pointless to advertise the articles

3. Which of the following is NOT true?

    A. Much money has been spent on advertising, so prices are greatly raised.

    B. Many people feel that the cost of advertising add to prices.

    C. Manufacturers feel that only a little amount is added to the price of each article.

4. A useful function of advertisements is _____.

    A. giving misinformation

    B. giving information

    C. leading to competition

5. "…people often complain that advertisements misinform rather than inform" can be paraphrased as "people often complain that they _____."

    A. cannot get any useful information from advertisements

    B. can get more useless information but less useful information

    C. usually get false instead of true information from advertisements

Unit Eighteen Advertising

 Grammar

让步从句(Clauses of Concession)总汇

1. 表示让步的介词(短语)

(1)for all (尽管,即使), in spite of, despite (尽管,即使), regardless of (不管,不顾)等介词(短语)后面均跟名词(短语);但 despite 不能与 of 连用。如:

He is a poor musician for all his training.
尽管他受过训练,但他仍然是个差劲的乐师。
In spite of this, she often appears on the stage as a young girl.
尽管如此,她经常在舞台上扮演姑娘。
We had a wonderful holiday in spite of / despite the weather.
尽管天气不好,我们还是过了一个十分愉快的假日。
All our proposals were rejected, regardless of their merits.
尽管我们的建议有其优点,但都被拒绝了。
He continued to speak, regardless of my feelings on the matter.
他不顾我对这个问题的感受接着往下讲。

(2)"In spite of/ Despite the fact that"结构也表示"尽管,虽然",但仅用于非常正式的文体中。如:

He came to the meeting despite the fact that he was seriously ill.
He came to the meeting although he was seriously ill.
尽管他病得很重,但他还是来开会了。

2. 表示让步的连接词

(1)表示让步的连接词有(al)though、even though / if, no matter ＋ who / when/ what/how…(不管谁/什么时候/什么/如何), whoever(不管谁), whenever(不管什么时候), whatever(不管什么), however(不管如何), for all that(尽管), while(虽然), 形容词/副词＋as / though(虽然), much as (虽然,尽管)等。如:

The farther away a thing is, the smaller it looks, even though it is really very big.
一个东西越远,看起来就越小,即使它实际上很大。
I wouldn't lose heart even if I should fail ten times.
纵然我失败10次,我也决不失去信心。
Though he was angry, he listened to me patiently.
他虽然很生气,但仍然耐心地听我说。
Although she had never been to Italy, she had heard a lot about it.
她虽然没有去过意大利,但却听过很多关于意大利的事。

(2)However / No matter how ＋形容词/副词＋主谓结构:

However hard he tried, he didn't succeed.（ however ＋副词＋主谓结构）
不管他已做了多大努力,他还是没成功。
No matter how busy you are, he always insists on coming with you.

不管你多忙，他总是非缠着你不可。(no matter how ＋形容词＋主谓结构)

(3)Whatever/Whichever（＝No matter what / which）＋名词＋主谓结构：

Whatever difficulties we meet, we complete our work in time.

不管我们会遇到什么困难，我们都将及时完成工作。

Whichever way he takes, he will be late for his plane.

不管他走哪条道，他都会误班机的。

(4)while 表示"虽然"时始终位于句首，如：

While I admit that the problems are difficult, I don't agree that they can't be solved.

虽然我承认这些问题很困难，但我并不同意这些问题解决不了。

(5)形容词/副词＋as / though（虽然）结构：

Bravely as / though they fought, they had no chance of winning.

虽然他们打得很勇敢，还是没有获胜的希望。

Much as I hated cruel sport, I couldn't help watching the boxing match.

尽管我讨厌残酷的运动项目，但我还是忍不住要观看拳击赛。

Fun time

1. All time is no time when it is past.
   机不可失，时不再来。
2. An apple a day keeps the doctor away.
   一日一个苹果，身体健康不求医。
3. A young idler, an old beggar.
   少壮不努力，老大徒伤悲。
4. Bad luck often brings good luck.
   塞翁失马，焉知非福。
5. Clumsy birds have to start flying early.
   笨鸟先飞，早入林。

单元复习

I 词汇练习

Choose the best choice for each of the following sentences.

1. I heard the news of your success _____ the radio.
   A. by   B. in   C. on
2. When he _____, Kate was already in the kitchen cooking breakfast.
   A. used up   B. woke up   C. put up

3. The snow and ice will soon _____ when the warm weather comes.
   A. die   B. occur   C. disappear
4. The workers guaranteed that no accident should _____ again.
   A. happened   B. come across   C. occur
5. In given circumstances, a bad thing can _____ good results.
   A. point to   B. lead to   C. go to
6. Because there is so much unemployment, the _____ for jobs is very fierce.
   A. choice   B. turn   C. competition
7. His charges were so ridiculous that it seemed _____ to answer him.
   A. pointless   B. meaningful   C. necessary
8. —What is the _____ of this diamond ring?
   —Seven hundred dollars.
   A. cost   B. price   C. spending
9. He _____ his voice so that everyone in the hall could hear what he was saying.
   A. raised   B. rose   C. hung
10. He has an income of 800 yuan a month but he spends only half that _____.
    A. number   B. total   C. amount
11. Different people have different _____ on the subject.
    A. views   B. points   C. thoughts
12. Though the conditions were hard, she never _____.
    A. complained B. thought   C. advanced

II 语法练习

Look at the example and join the two sentences together by using the attributive clause.

Example: This machine is still working perfectly. I have looked after this machine for twenty years.
This machine which I have looked after for twenty years is still working perfectly.

1. They were always on the move. This made it very difficult to get in contact with them.

2. He advised me to go and see his sister. She might be able to do something to help.

3. We test every sample in our laboratories. That is why it is so reliable.

4. They take good care of Aunt Liu. Her son gave his life for the people during the War of Liberation.

5. The child is living with his aunt. His parents died in the air crash.

6. He gave special help to some students. Their pronunciation was not so good.

7. The girl learnt to play the piano when she was a small child. Her father is a famous pianist.

_____

8. The fire started on the first floor of the hospital. Many of its patients are elderly people.

_____

Ⅲ 阅读理解

Read the passage and choose the best answer for each of the questions from the four choices.

  The cinema was in darkness when we went in and it was no easy job making our way to our seats. An old man was walking in front of us. He was lucky as he had a stick to help him find his way, just like a blind man.

  "It's funny not to have any light on before the film begins," I said. "And not music, either," added my wife. "Well, perhaps they want to save electricity." We were in one of the rows near the entrance when we heard other people pass by. But we could not tell how many people were at cinema. It was usually much crowded at this time of the day.

  "It must be 2 o'clock already," my wife said, getting restless. "Can you see your watch?"

  My eyes had now got used to the darkness and by bringing my watch close to my eyes, I could just make out that it was a little after two.

  Just then the film started, but we were disappointed to find that there had been a change. It was not the film we wanted to see. They were showing an old film. My wife and I had seen it three times in the past two months!

1. We got to the cinema _____ the film started.

    A. before   B. after   C. soon after   D. as soon as

2. The film should start _____.

    A. before 2:00   B. after 2:00   C. at 2:00   D. around 2:00

3. Usually before the film starts, there should be _____ in the cinema.

    A. many people   B. an old man

    C. light and music   D. darkness

4. It seems that the cinema is more crowded _____.

    A. early in the afternoon   B. late in the afternoon

    C. at two o'clock   D. early in the morning

5. We were disappointed that _____.

    A. we didn't see a film

    B. we had to walk in darkness to see a new film

    C. there was no music or light in the cinema

    D. the film was not the one that we want to see

138